Survival Guide For Empaths

How To Overcome Your Limiting Beliefs, A Plan For The Highly Sensitive, Coping With Distress, Empath Healing Made Easy For Beginners

Kristine S. Everest

Survival Guide For Empaths: How To Overcome Your Limiting Beliefs, A Plan For The Highly Sensitive, Coping With Distress, Empath Healing Made Easy For Beginners

Table of Contents

Book 1 - Overcome Your Limiting Beliefs..................................1

1 - Introduction...2

2 - What are limiting beliefs?...5

    The Belief that Empaths Have No Control Over What They Feel
....6

    The Belief that Empaths are Merely Individuals that are Too
Emotional..10

3 - The Belief that Empaths are Intruders.........................15

4 - The Belief that Other People Will Find Empaths as
Freaks...19

5 - The Belief that One is not Strong Enough to be an Em-
path...22

6 - The Belief that Empaths are Pushovers.......................25

7 - The Belief that People Will Reject You.........................27

8 - The Belief that Nobody Else Understands....................30

9 - The Belief that Empaths are Dumping Ground for Oth-
ers...34

10 - The Belief that Empaths Cannot Handle Romantic Relationships..37

11 - The Belief that Empaths are Emotionally Imbalanced. 41

12 - The Belief that Empaths become Addicts....................44

13 - The Belief that Empaths are Psychologically Frail.......48

14 - The Belief that Empaths who are Unable to Repel Negativity are Weak..51

15 - The Belief that Empaths Cannot Function in the Work-
place...55

16 - Breaking Free of Limiting Beliefs..............................59

    Self-Awareness...59

    Shielding..60

    Cleansing..61

    Meditation..63

    Setting Boundaries..64

    Take a Bath...65

    Connecting with Others..66

17 - Conclusion..67

Book 2 - A Plan For The Highly Sensitive..........................68

1 - Introduction...69

2 - The HSP Empath Defined...71

What are the characteristics of HSPs?.................................72
3 - HSP characteristics are summarized with the acronym DOES.................................73
Depth of Processing.................................73
Overstimulated.................................74
Emotionally Reactive.................................74
Sensitive to Subtle Stimuli.................................75
4 - High Sensitivity Is Not.................................76
A Disorder.................................76
Shyness.................................76
Introversion.................................76
Why There Are Highly Sensitive People.................................77
Signs of Being an HSP.................................79
What are Empaths?.................................84
Why There Are Empaths.................................85
5 - Signs of Being an Empath.................................87
Differentiating HSPs and Empaths.................................89
Pros and Cons of being an HSP and Empath.................................91
HSP Brainwaves.................................94
6 - Coping Techniques for the HSP Empath.................................96
Health.................................96
Food and Drink.................................97
Environment.................................98
Other People.................................99
Talk with Someone Who Understands.................................101
Stimulation.................................101
Routines.................................102
Time Management.................................104
Traveling.................................105
Relaxing.................................105
Identify What Makes You Uncomfortable and Plan What to Do with Them.................................106
Look for Things that Energize You.................................107
Focus on Positive Things When You're Down.................................108
Keep Yourself Busy.................................108
Stay in Nature.................................109
Have Kind Words for Yourself.................................109
Coping with Indecisiveness.................................109
Know What You Are Afraid Of.................................110
Forget What You "Should" Do.................................110
Do Not Give in to Analysis Paralysis.................................110
Give Yourself Time.................................111
Pretend that You Have Already Decided.................................111
Stay Away from Draining Situations.................................112
Avoid People Who Drain You.................................113
Set Boundaries.................................113

Like Yourself..114
Be Selective of Your Companions.............................114
Be More Expressive...115
Problem Solving..115

7 - Managing Criticisms...117
Refuse to be labeled..117
If you're at fault, acknowledge it and apologize appropriately. 117
Ask for clarification..117
Giving Complaints...118
Name the problem..118
State your feelings..118
Specify what you want...119
Ask for reasonable changes one at a time so that others can
manage to do it..119

8 - Keeping Emotions at a Manageable Level.............120
Meditate...120
Calm Down...121
Modify Your Perspective...121
Focus On What's Important...121
Fake It..122
Process It...122
Express What You Feel...122
Enhance Positive Emotions...123
Changing your belief also changes your reactions.....128
Alter Your Memories...128
Lessening the Effect of Negative Memories...............129
Changing Your Feelings..129
Control your Inner Voice...129
Meditation for the HSP Empath..................................130
Reciting Affirmations..131
Focusing on an Object...134
Focusing on an Idea...134
Mindfulness...135
Breathing Meditation..136
Heartbeat Meditation..137
Sensing..137
Music Meditation...138
Visualizing...138
Facilitating Success...139
Writing...139
Progressive Relaxation..140
Mental Relaxation...141
Moving Meditations...141
Detachment..142
Watching Thoughts..143
Koans...143

Knowing the Knower..144
9 - Conclusion...146
Book 3 - Coping With Distress...148
1 - Introduction...149
2 - Defining an Empath...151
The Characteristics of an Empath.......................................152
The Life Of An Empath...154
3 - Stress and the Empath...156
What is stress?..156
Where does stress come from?...159
Empath Stress...160
Second-Hand Stress...161
The Empath's Defenses...163
Distance..163
Loving Yourself..164
4 - Creativity...167
Shielding..167
Mental Imagery..168
5 - Boundary Setting...172
Mindfulness Meditation..174
6 - Protective Clothing...177
Silk..177
Mirrors...177
Empath Magic...178
Zooming In..178
Junking the Routine..180
Simmer Down at Night...181
Check Yourself Constantly...181
Bedtime Fun..182
Pool Time...183
Terrific Tea..184
Humor...185
The Hand Rub...186
Pet Magic...187
Regaining Control..188
7 - Alternative Remedies for Empaths.............................190
Acupuncture..190
What is Acupuncture?..190
Acupuncture for Empaths...191
Music Therapy..192
Weightless – Marconi Union..193
Aromatherapy...194
Hypnosis..196
Professional Hypnosis..197
Self-Hypnosis..197

Color Therapy...201
8 - Dealing with Emotional Vampires.............................204
    What is an emotional vampire?................................204
    The Five Vampires..205
9 - Conclusion..214
Book 4 - Empath Healing Made Easy For Beginners........215
1 - Introduction..216
    What Is Empathy?...216
    Empathy..216
    Healer...216
    Empathy and Healing: The Connection...................216
    Empathy is inherited..218
2 - Different Levels of Being an Empath........................219
    Psychometry..219
    Telepathy..219
    Physical Healing..219
    Emotional Healing...220
    Animal Communication...220
    Nature...220
    Precognition...220
    Claircognizance...221
3 - Common Empathic Traits...222
    Knowing..222
4 - Being Empathic and the Ability to Heal...................231
5 - What to Avoid if you are an empath.........................233
6 - Self-Care for Empathic People.................................234
7 - Energy Techniques for the Intuitive Feeler..............238
    The Zip Up..238
    Creating a Shield of Light...240
    Belly Breathing..242
8 - Lifestyle Changes for Empaths.................................244
9 - Tips for Curing Emotional Hangovers......................248
    Shower meditation..248
    Light a white-colored candle....................................249
    Aromatherapy..249
    Nature...249
    Create your sanctuary..250
10 - Empaths and the Workplace...................................251
    Observing Body Language Cues................................255
    Pay Attention to Appearance...................................256
    Notice Posture...257
    Watch For Physical Movements................................257
    Pay attention to people's hands...............................258
    Lip biting..258

Interpreting Facial Expressions..259
Listen to Your Intuition..259
Checklist of Intuitive Cues..260
Sense Emotional Energy...261

11 - Strategies to Read Emotional Energy......................263
Sense People's Presence..263
Watch people's eyes..263
Notice the feel of a handshake, hug, and touch.............264
Listen for people's laughter and tone of voice...............264

12 - The Connection Between Diet and Empathy.............266
So why do empaths have sensitive bodies, and systems?........266
Fatty Fish...268
Whole Grains...269
Lean Protein..269
Leafy Greens..270
Mood Foods: How Amino Acids Feed Your Brain.............270

13 - Restoring Energy and Focus...................................272
Boosting Your Ability to Relax.....................................273
Food vs. Comfort..273
Serotonin, the All-Natural Prozac.................................275

14 - Inspiring Change by Using Your Empathic Abilities..277
Cultivate Your Curiosity..277
Step Into Someone Else's Shoes....................................278
Inspiring Social Change...280

Thank You..283
Disclaimer..284

Book 1 - Overcome Your Limiting Beliefs

How To Overcome Your Limiting Beliefs (Survival Guide, Strategies for Sensitive People, Emotional Healing, How To Thrive)

1 - Introduction

Being an empath is not an easy thing. Your high sensitivity to the energy emanating around you can be quite overwhelming at times. You feel what other people are feeling which can create havoc with your own emotions.

But despite these seemingly uncontrollable waves of energy that engulf you, being an empath is a gift. Once you learn the proper tools to protect yourself, you can do a lot of good in the world.

Your ability to sense what others are feeling makes you an extraordinary person. There are numerous benefits to being a highly sensitive person which include the following.

Empaths are natural healers. Your positive energy can do wonders for the psyche of people around you. Your friends and family (and sometimes even strangers) feel better when they talk to you or even just sit beside you. You provide others with peace of mind to help them deal with their own issues.

Empaths are not afraid to be alone. In fact, you welcome the opportunity of being by yourself. But this doesn't mean that you are a loner. You just don't feel the same fear that everyone else does at the thought of not being around anybody.

You crave those moments of silence and find yourself feeling more relaxed after your moments of solitude.

Empaths are extremely creative. You can express your feelings and ideas in different mediums. However, your creativity is not limited to just the arts. You have the capacity and ability to deal with difficult situations by using your own unique approach.

You see the world from a different perspective which allows you to find solutions that others wouldn't normally think of. People may often find your unconventional methods eccentric but you manage to get things done.

Empaths can notice non-verbal clues. People don't need to talk about what they're feeling, you already know. You immediately sense whether they are sad or happy despite their outward expressions. You know if their laughter is simply a facade to cover up what they are truly feeling.

And because of this it is extremely difficult for people to lie to you. You have a heightened awareness of their emotions and thoughts so you are often able to address what they need even if they try to hide it.

Empaths understand the world they live in. Your ability to

sense energy is not limited to people. You can feel it emanating from nature and even inanimate objects. You feel better and even stronger when surrounded by nature.

Empaths have a heightened sense of smell. You may have noticed how you seem to be able to smell the odor of everything around you more intensely than others. Hence, eating, drinking, and even just taking a walk around the garden is a lot more pleasant for you. Some Empaths even develop their skill of picking up scents to the point that they can smell illnesses and even death.

However, despite all these great things that you get by being an empath, there are highly sensitive people who never reach their full potential. And these are because of the limiting beliefs that hold them down.

2 - What are limiting beliefs?

These are ideas that constrain you because you believe them to be the absolute truth. These are developed because of events or triggers that happen in your life. As an empath, these limiting beliefs can either be about your capacity to handle your gift or about how others will perceive you.

And because you accept these as the truth, you find yourself unable to develop and increase the power of your special abilities. These beliefs also affect the quality of life you lead. You become a recluse and develop bad habits just to be able to deal.

For example, you are afraid that when people find out what you can do, they might think you're a freak. This is of course not something that anyone would feel happy about. To protect yourself, you hide your gift. You either retreat from social interactions or just choose to shut out what you can do.

This book contains the limiting beliefs that most empaths have. It explains how each one impacts your ability as a highly sensitive person. Its goal is to help you understand and overcome these beliefs so you can lead a happier and healthier life as an Empath. This book also contains different tools that you can use to protect yourself.

The Belief that Empaths Have No Control Over What They Feel

For as long as you can remember you've always been sensitive to how others around you were feeling. When you were younger, you couldn't understand why you would suddenly feel elated or sad for no reason at all.

You were also puzzled by how hanging around certain people made you feel extremely tired even if all you did was sit and talk. These were all mysteries that finally made sense when you found out that you were an empath or highly sensitive person.

Unfortunately, this discovery certainly did not make things easier. You did finally know the reason behind all the unusual feelings and emotions that would suddenly overcome you. But you also found out that because of your ability, you will forever be plagued by the overwhelming energy that you sense almost everywhere you go.

You walk into a room full of people and the rush of thoughts and emotions can sometimes leave you reeling in shock. You feel almost everything while it feels like a ton of bricks fell on you. Whatever your mood is before you walked in is completely gone and is replaced by whatever everybody else is feeling.

You swing from one emotion to another without any logical explanation. You go from being ecstatic to being worried then sad in a matter of minutes. And because of this you find yourself dreading interacting with other people. Being around friends or family becomes a struggle and you end up being perceived as eccentric or moody.

Despite wanting to be with people you care for, you realize that your ability is holding you back. You get intense headaches and often feel exhausted when you're with others. Even simple things such as watching the news or a movie produces such powerful emotional surges in you. All you want to do is crawl under a blanket and hide from the world.

Finding out you are an empath made you realize that you have absolutely no control over your ability. It isn't like a tap you can turn on and off whenever convenient. And because of this, you resent being a highly sensitive person. You wish nothing more than to be a normal person.

Believing that you have no control over your life because of your gift stops you from realizing your full potential. Instead of embracing your ability, you retreat from social gatherings. You also often lose touch with the outside world because you avoid seeing anything that can cause intense reactions. You surrender to the fact that that there is nothing you can do but hide.

But being highly sensitive to the energy of the universe around you does not mean that you no longer have power over your life. Your abilities put you in charge. While it is true that you cannot control how other people feel or think, you do have a say in how it will affect you.

Accepting that you are an empath is not raising the white flag and opening yourself up to suffering. Coming to terms with your gift means you can start taking measures to protect yourself. There are various ways for you to thrive and live a healthier life as an empath.

One of these ways is called shielding.

Shielding is when you visualize a wall or force field around you. This wall is your way of keeping the emotions of people out. While it may seem like just a figment of the imagination, visualization is highly effective. And the more solid this visualized wall is, the more protection it can give you.

To make shielding more effective you also need to know yourself. Before you go out, take an inventory of what you really feel. Are you happy? Are you worried about something? By knowing what emotions are really yours will help you deal with the energy that you will be picking up once you are with company.

When you start feeling sad, ask yourself what it is in your life that may be causing you to feel this way. If there is no logical reason for you to be sad, tell yourself that it is not your own emotion and simply something that you are picking up from somebody else. And once you identify that the emotion is not yours, visualize it being ejected to the other side of your shield.

You are an empath. It means you can sense the energy around you. It also means you can control how it affects you as an individual. So, take the reins and let go of the belief that your gift turns you into an unwilling human energy sponge. One you learn how to protect yourself, you can use your abilities as a highly sensitive person to do a lot of good.

The Belief that Empaths are Merely Individuals that are Too Emotional

Today's society boasts of being open and diverse. Unfortunately, despite these claims, being different is still a struggle. People tend to be unforgiving to what they don't understand. There are dictated norms that everybody is expected to follow. And when you don't conform, you often find yourself being an outcast.

When you first began to sense your abilities, you were told that it was something else other than what it truly is. People around you tried to explain what you were going through without understanding what it really was.

When you told people that you could feel their emotions they feared that you would reveal what they truly felt beneath their facade. So, to feel better they told you that you had an overactive imagination. They claim that it was all in your head, that you were given to flights of fancy.

When you were a child, you may have even been told to stop watching too much TV. What you thought you were feeling was simply an effect of all the shows you saw where superheroes could read minds. And despite how much you tried to explain that it wasn't reading or hearing but rather sensing their emotions, you were immediately shot down.

And when people saw how long it took for you to get over seeing something sad, they called you over-emotional. They were confused at how you could be moved to tears and feel emotionally drained by just watching. You may have experienced embarrassing moments when you simply could not control yourself when watching sad scenes in movies or on TV.

Sure, everybody else was tearing up because one of the main characters had gotten hurt. But by the time the credits rolled, all the folks around you had moved on. You, on the other hand, could just not let go of the feeling of loss. It was as if you were the one whose loved one had died.

At the beginning, people were sympathetic. But the more they saw you reacting intensely to even just fictional situations, the more they could not understand. You were told to stop being too sensitive and to simply move on. People started finding you a bit over dramatic and began to feel uncomfortable around you. This just made the situation so much worse because you could sense everything they were feeling.

While most of the assumptions that people had about you were not always meant to hurt or ridicule, you began to believe they were all true. You too started believing that the only reason you felt the way you did was because you were simply too sensitive.

It was not a special ability. It was merely a character flaw that you would eventually grow out of. All you had to do learn to let it go. It was okay to feel uncomfortable when seeing something violent on the news, but being physically sick was not.

You remain conflicted with the ideas that you have been made to believe and what you go through every single day. If it truly was just your imagination, then why do you feel exhausted when you're around certain people? Why is it that when somebody is hurt, you feel the same pain they are going through? Why do you cry buckets and buckets of tears for no reason at all?

But because you have been convinced that what you feel is all in your mind, you don't find any reason to further develop it. So, despite feeling like your drowning in the strong energy that you pick up, you tell yourself you are just like everybody else. There is nothing special about what you are going through. As a result, various aspects of your life suffer.

You have a strained relationship with the people that you interact with. You find yourself unable to assert yourself as you feel guilty when others feel bad. You are unable to function properly especially around certain people. They make you feel uncomfortable with the energy they exude. They in return tend to be wary of you.

There are people though who are unexplainably drawn to you. You start becoming their emotional baggage counter. They unload on you any problems or dilemmas they are going through because you just make them feel better. You end up feeling tired to the point of exhaustion.

You also have quite a few health conditions. You have chronic fatigue and intense headaches that even escalate to migraine attacks. You tend to be clumsy especially when you're around a lot of people. It's the reason you often have bumps, bruises, and scratches. You also feel out of balance most of the time.

In addition, you get physically sick when you see violence even if it's just in a movie or on TV. You find yourself crying for no reason at all. Because you don't accept that you have a gift, you end up experiencing intense low moments. You get inexplicably depressed and it takes you forever to snap out of it.

All these are happening to you just because you were told that what you were feeling were not real. You were simply too emotional. Your unhealthy overactive imagination triggers irrational emotional responses. So, instead of becoming a stronger empath, you become afraid and confused.

The first step to living a healthier life is to believe that you are blessed with abilities that make you special. And these abilities are supposed to be developed and not denied. Once you do this, you can start living a more productive and fruitful life.

3 - The Belief that Empaths are Intruders

People wear masks for a variety of reasons. Some mask their sadness with a happy expression to stop others from worrying about them. Some put on a more confident façade to hide their insecurities. Whether it is to gain a more favorable social standing or a need to keep their true emotions inside, people wear masks to be able to be able to cope with everyday life. It is part of human nature.

Being an empath means you can see beneath the masks that people wear. You can sense the emotions that others try to keep from the rest of the world. For example, a friend at work tells you that they are excited about being promoted.

But when you're around this person what you can feel is an intense fear of failure. Despite his confident outward appearance, you know, without him saying anything that he doesn't feel up to the job.

Your ability to see through people's facade often makes you feel like an intruder. It's like eavesdropping on a personal conversation. There is a reason they choose to keep it to themselves and you see exactly what they want to hide. Without their masks, people feel naked and vulnerable.

Your gift puts them in that situation every time they are around you.

As an empath. you feel guilty about knowing what they are feeling. As a result, you often try to overcompensate. You tend to treat them with kids gloves and this may sometimes be perceived as threatening. Without their permission, you have access to personal matters that you feel you should not be entrusted with.

This feeling of guilt at intruding other people's personal space makes you feel that your gift is a sin. You have no right to intrude upon other people's business and especially not with their emotions. You feel even more stricken because sensing their emotions and energy is something that comes innately. You do not do it deliberately, that's just how you are.

Your perception that you are intruding doesn't just stem from guilt. As an Empath, it is in your nature to try and fix things. Because you know how horrible they feel, you find ways to help them overcome whatever it is that people are struggling with. Some folks welcome your attempt to make things better, but others feel offended.

They do not want anybody else to know what they are feeling. It was the reason they chose to put up masks in the first place. Finding out that you can tell that they are not being truthful can make them feel exposed. They lash out and tell you to keep your nose out of their business.

Their anger and resentment hits you quite hard. Because you are highly sensitive to their energy and can feel their emotions as though these were your own, you start to feel angry as well. The result, of course, is not very pretty.

And because of all these, you feel that you are doing something wrong. You decide not to tap into your abilities. You are afraid that developing it further will be even more damaging to you and the people around you. You resent that you know exactly what is going on and find it a huge burden to always know the truth.

You retreat into your own world. You try to ignore the energy around you. But all it does is make you feel guiltier. It almost seems like you're watching someone about to fall but do nothing to save them. Guilt and feeling that you are an intruder limit your potential as an empath.

However, there are tools that you can use to manage your

abilities better. You can keep the emotions of others from affecting you by shielding yourself. You also need to set up boundaries so you don't try to be the superhero in everybody's lives. You will need to accept that there are people you can help, people who actually want your help. But there are also those who you will need to let go.

To stop feeling like an intruder, you need to come to terms with the fact that you are only picking up on what is being put out there. You don't pick out specific people and you don't do it to serve your own purpose. The main reason you can sense what other folks feel is because you are in tune with the energy of everything around you.

4 - The Belief that Other People Will Find Empaths as Freaks

Having a special ability can be awesome, that is if your life was a movie or TV show. Gifts such as being able to sense what others around you feel and think is not as amazing in real life. You're not considered a superhero. You are perceived as quite the opposite. In some cases, you might even be thought of as having mental problems.

The real world does not embrace abilities such as being an empath. There are folks who would think that you were a candidate to the funny farm if you told them what you could do. Letting others know that you are highly sensitive to the energy of the universe is almost the same as running around in a costume and saying you can fly.

There are those though who will believe you. But it's not a walk into the sunset or happily ever after when people know about your gift. You would be treated differently and this is something that you absolutely dread. You know you are not normal, but you certainly do not want to be considered abnormal.

What makes it even more unbearable is that you can tell exactly how they feel about you. Some well-meaning friends may tell you that they're okay with what you can do but you may sense something else. You may pick up fear and resentment. Being able to see through their reassuring statements just makes you feel more like a freak than ever.

Your fear of ever being perceived as a weirdo prevents you from fully embracing being an Empath. After all, you are only human and despite your abilities, you are certainly not happy at being considered a freak. Hence, you go against your nature of helping others or trying to help people heal.

You try to avoid being around too many people. The less social interaction you have the fewer chances of showing any sign of what you can do. For example, you choose not to go to parties as a roomful of folks is a nightmare. Just imagine all the energy, thoughts, and feelings that you would pick up with so many people around you.

Normal people don't sense the energy of the universe. They don't feel what other people are feeling to the point of physical pain. They can relate to what others are going through. But they certainly don't inexplicably experience the same exact emotions.

So, if your ability isn't something that normal people have, that would mean you aren't normal. And you are terrified of people finding out. Your attempt to take control of your ability without the proper training makes you appear aloof and distant

Because of this, you chose not to nurture your gift. You attempt to keep it a secret instead of reaching out for help. Without the right guidance, you will not be able to develop your abilities to its full potential which means you leave yourself vulnerable.

All the emotions and energy that you pick up will have a negative effect on your health. You'll suffer from ailments such as chronic headaches and fatigue. This belief that other people will think you are a freak certainly has an impact on your Empathic abilities and the quality of life you lead.

5 - The Belief that One is not Strong Enough to be an Empath

"With great power comes great responsibility" Nobody can relate to that popular movie line better than you. With your ability to sense the energy that the world around you exudes, it means you also have a responsibility to use it to help. You have a purpose but isn't one that you think you will be able to fulfill.

When a roomful of people surrounds you, you pick up multiple emotions in varying degrees. The effect of all these can be quite overwhelming. You seesaw from one emotion to another.

It is draining and can mess up your own psyche. There's a reason human beings don't experience all sorts of emotions at the same time. One can't be happy, sad, afraid, elated and anxious all at the same time. And one can't transition from one to another in a matter of seconds.

Events trigger emotions. For an individual to feel anything, a physical or psychological change needs to happen. For example, if a person watches a movie where someone dies, he or she may feel sad. That person can relate to the feeling of loss that the character in the movie feels. But as an empath, you don't just relate to the emotion. You feel like you are the one who suffered the loss.

Other people cannot even begin to imagine what it's like to be around others and feel exactly what they are feeling. If one person in the room is sad and the other is angry, you notice both emotions at the same time. And because you have no triggers to explain the change in your mood, it can sometimes fccl like you are going mad. Without the proper guidance, you are left defenseless.

While your gifts as an Empath are innate, the ability to protect yourself isn't. And this makes you feel like you are too weak to handle everything that you pick up. Human nature makes you reject that which you cannot understand. You either chose to stay away from other people or just let the emotions get their way.

Even if there was no reason for you to be angry, you lashed out with the intense rage that you picked up. There were also moments when you just drowned in sadness. You felt depressed because you couldn't manage the inexplicable sorrow that engulfs you.

The belief that you are not strong enough is a serious handicap that prevents you from embracing your gift. You simply assume that you are being able to sense the energy around you is a bad joke that the universe is playing on you. And you are certainly not amused.

Unfortunately, this means you do not see the potential of your abilities. Your gift as an empath does not get nurtured. It also has a negative impact on the quality of life you lead.

Instead of being able to help others, you find yourself alienating those you interact with. You constantly feel drained when you're with company. You don't see yourself as being a strong person emotionally as it takes you forever to get over anything. And because you feel like a victim most of the time, you don't seek out help.

As a result, you don't grow as an empath. You get stuck with simply being an individual who appears moody and not in control of their own emotions. For Highly Sensitive People like you, this can be quite tragic. You don't get to do what you were born to do and often feel ostracized by society.

6 - The Belief that Empaths are Pushovers

Your ability to function well in society is affected by the belief that being an empath makes you a pushover. Because you can sense the energy around you, you have difficulty acting in a manner that would benefit you.

For example, when somebody asks you to do something for them, you find it difficult to say no. And this is because you hate having to be the reason behind the disappointment they feel when you do. This makes you feel guilty.

Guilt then makes you give in to something that you would not have wanted to do. Once you are no longer in that other person's presence, you hate that you were not strong enough to stand your own ground. But being sensitive to the emotions of others does not necessarily mean that you are a pushover. With the right tools, you can thrive in any social interaction.

One of the challenges that you face every single day is that you are sensitive to the energy around you. And by being sensitive, it basically means that you pick up emotions, feelings, and thoughts from anything and anybody that you interact with. You don't just relate to what they're going through, you share the experience. And because you do, you try to find ways to make everything better.

This sometimes results in you giving in to others or spending too much of your energy to help. Therefore, you often feel so exhausted. You also tend to feel resentful of your ability. But being an Empath does not mean that you should surrender yourself to feeling burdened by your gift. With the right tools, you can function properly in any social setting.

Letting go of your belief that being an empath and pushover are synonymous is the first step. You need to believe that you can help others without giving up your own voice or compromising your own well-being. There are various methods that you can learn to be able to live a more fulfilling life as an Empath.

These methods include visualization and meditation. Visualizing helps you protect yourself while meditation allows you to recharge your energy. But the only way that these will work is if you embrace your gift. Accepting that your abilities do not limit your life is crucial.

7 - The Belief that People Will Reject You

A limiting belief that holds you back from living a fulfilling life is the fear of rejection. It's not easy being different. People fear what they don't understand. Your abilities as an empath are certainly something that even you yourself found hard to understand.

And because of this, you believe that others will not be able to accept you and your gift. Nobody will want to be around somebody who can see beyond the emotional wall that they put up to protect themselves.

Psychology explains that the reason people choose to show a different facade to what they feel is for self-preservation. We choose to appear confident when we are scared or happy when we are really scared.

Some folks are more scheming though. They put up a show of weakness to catch others by surprise. As an empath, you can see through these pretenses. Sadly, because you know how threatening this can be to other people, you too put up your own defensive wall.

You choose not to let others know about what you can do.

You are afraid that when your friends and family and even strangers will give you a wide berth. You believe that your gift is like a disease that will drive people away. While you're not afraid of being on your own, you despise the thought of being treated as a pariah.

What makes it even worse is that even if others hide how they feel about your abilities, you can sense the truth. This creates awkward social interactions. They know that you know how they really feel and it's like walking on eggshells.

And it is for this reason that you hide or deny that you are an empath. This denial isn't just for the sake of others. You also try to convince yourself that everything you are sensing is just figments of your imagination. You make yourself believe that if you ignore it, the emotions and feelings will just go away.

Sadly, this fear of rejection will stop you from finding ways to nurture your gift. You won't reach out to those who can help you because you are certain that coming out as an empath is the worst thing that can happen to you. Because of this, your abilities will be limited. You won't be able to grow as a highly sensitive person and will always have mixed feelings on how to handle your abilities.

But while it is true that there may be people who will be put off by what you can do, harnessing your gift isn't something that you need to be afraid of. Being an empath is similar to being highly skilled at something. There are people who can draw well. There are those that can calculate ridiculous amounts of numbers in their heads. Your expertise is on tuning into the energy around you.

This ability will allow you to help others come to terms with their own fears. You will be able to help people deal with their difficulties and heal themselves. Your presence alone often makes people feel better. And if you would just let go of the fear of rejection, there is so much good that you can do.

Whether you stay in the closet as an Empath or choose to be open about it, you will never be able to please everybody. For someone like you, this can be quite painful. Just keep in mind that despite any early confusion or even fear, the people who truly matter will accept you. People fear what they do not understand. That is true. But the first step in making them understand is to embrace your own gift.

8 - The Belief that Nobody Else Understands

As an empath, you see the world differently. Your perception of things and people are quite unique. And this is because you have access to something that nobody else does. You can sense the energy emanating around you. You can sense what people are feeling and even what plants and animals around you need.

You can walk past the window of a pet store and feel unbelievably sad when you see the animals in cages. While others beside you are busy cooing at the cute puppies and kittens, you sense something else entirely. You know if any of the animals are hungry, hurting or sad, so, you react differently.

When you're around sick people, something unusual happens to you. You start feeling the same aches and pains that they're feeling. You know that if you tell other folks about what you're going through, they would think that you're just making it up. It will come across as though you're just looking for attention.

Another thing that you experience as an empath is your amplified reaction to anything you see or watch. For example, when you watch the news, you feel overly depressed and sad at the state of the world. You see people hurt in wars or accidents and it just makes you physically ill.

While these scenes may be unsettling for any regular person, the effects on you are just overwhelming. And therefore, it takes you so much longer to get over seeing anything violent or sad.

You know that not everybody can sense the same energy that you do. You see that while people can relate to how others feel, they don't physically experience the same pain or emotion. You have accepted that you are different.

Sadly, you also believe that there is no way other folks can understand you. How can they when they have no idea what you are going through? You worry that you will be perceived as odd and perhaps even mentally disturbed.

Believing that other people will not be able to understand what you are experiencing will limit your growth as an Empath. When you feel that there is no one you can talk to about what you can do, you tend to retreat from others. You keep your abilities a secret. You might even deny that you are an empath when asked.

You shut out the emotions that you sense in the hopes to hide your abilities to others. As a result, you appear cold and distant. Other people then feel wary or uncomfortable around you. As an empath, you can feel these negative energies and get affected by these.

Your interpersonal relationships then become even more strained because you're trying to conceal your gift. You appear moody and distant. You come across as someone who just broods and sulks whenever something unpleasant happens.

And because you choose to stay quiet about what you can do, it becomes even harder for other people to understand you. You don't let people get too close to you because you are certain that they will not be able to understand you.

You are sure that because they don't have the same abilities that you do, it will be impossible for them to see things the way you do. To prevent yourself from getting hurt, you opt to just deal with everything on your own.

Your belief that no one else could possibly understand you and what you can do just makes things even more difficult for you. It stops you from being able to socialize with others in any type of setting. It certainly affects the quality of life that you lead.

The first step in thriving as an empath is to accept that being different isn't a bad thing. It is not your abilities that hold you back from having successful relationships with friends and family. It is your fear of not being accepted and understood that becomes an obstacle. Embracing your gift and learning the different tools to help you manage your abilities is the key.

There are various empath organizations that you can reach out to for guidance. Communicating with other Highly Sensitive People will certainly be able to help you deal with everyday challenges that you encounter. From protecting yourself from the onslaught of emotions to keeping yourself healthy, these organizations have something useful to share.

9 - The Belief that Empaths are Dumping Ground for Others

One of the benefits that Empaths offer other people is that they can absorb negative energy. Most people who confide in you feel a lot better after being with you. And this is even without you offering any words of advice or comfort. Just merely being in your presence gives people who are anxious or going through a difficult time temporary relief.

This is the reason people are attracted to you. Even if they don't know that you are an Empath, they are naturally drawn to you because of how much better you make them feel. Unfortunately, being the dumping ground of other people's emotional baggage isn't healthy for you.

You may have noticed how drained you feel whenever you interact with people who are going through difficult times. And this is because you unintentionally share your positive energy with them and take the negative one that they are giving off.

Because of the exchange of energy, empaths like you, often suffer from chronic ailments such as fatigue and migraines. And of course, this affects the quality of life that you lead. Sadly, most empaths believe that making others feel better

9 - THE BELIEF THAT EMPATHS ARE DUMPING GROUND FOR OTHERS

is their duty.

They believe that it is their purpose and have no choice but to fulfill it. If you feel this way, then you raise the white flag and surrender to a life where you act as dumping ground for others.

The result is either you give in and accept the baggage or you turn into a recluse. However, despite your willingness to help, you do eventually veer towards the latter.

You find yourself turning away from friends who are going through tough times because you can no longer handle the physical exhaustion of helping them out. You also become reluctant to meet new folks. You dread that they too may begin feeling the urge to unload on you.

This belief that becoming someone's confidant is inevitable holds you back from realizing your full potential as an empath. You feel that you have absolutely no control and end up a victim of your gift. However, there are different methods that you can use to protect yourself. One of these methods is choosing who you can help.

There are two types of people who come to you for help. The

first type is the ones who have tried to overcome their difficulties on their own. They take charge of their lives and only really come to you for a moment of calm. They don't expect you to solve things for them but being with you does give them the energy to continue.

The second type is the folks who tend to spread misery. They complain and see themselves as victims. They don't do anything to try to fix their problems and choose to keep talking about what they're going through with other people.

They don't listen to advice as they don't plan to act. They will keep repeating how unlucky they are and how life has dealt them a bad deal. You cannot help this type of person as they do not really want it. All they're looking for is someone to feel as miserable as they do.

When you're around people who try to unload on you, you do have a choice. Being an Empath doesn't mean that you no longer have the right to say no. It does take a bit of work for you though. Choose who you can help and toughen up and say no to the ones you can't. They might become upset or disappointed but to be able to help more people, you will need to turn some down.

10 - The Belief that Empaths Cannot Handle Romantic Relationships

Empaths come across as loners. But you know that the opposite is true. While you do crave solitude to escape from the overwhelming surge of energy that you sense, you still search for someone to share your life with. You are just like everybody else. You need someone to love and to love you back.

However, because of your high sensitivity, you are afraid that you may not be able to handle a romance. Platonic relationships are already hard, imagine how much more difficult it would be to fall in love.

Some people might think that your ability makes it easier to have a partner. After all, you'll already know what they need which makes you an ideal boyfriend or girlfriend. Unfortunately, you believe that your gift will just overcomplicate everything.

You can sense when somebody is lying. How challenging would that be, if the person who's not being entirely truthful is your partner? You would be torn between admitting that you know the truth and respecting boundaries. Another difficulty that you face is how to resolve conflicts.

If you disagree or fight over something, you may tend to give in without discussing what the issue is. You dislike sensing anger or sadness from your partner, so you may decide to just forget about whatever it was that you were arguing about.

As a result, you will both agree to just not talk about 'it' anymore. However, the problem starts when you begin having more 'it' in your relationship. There would be so much that you don't talk about that you may just end up not talking at all.

As an empath, this would be unbearable for you. You would hate the silence and the lack of communication. You can sense what your partner is feeling but are held back by your agreement to not talk about touchy subjects.

You are convinced that your gift just makes it harder for you to enjoy a romantic relationship. Sadly, people assume that you don't need that type of intimacy. Your manner of relating to others creates the impression that you would rather be alone.

But as an empath, it is in your nature to want to be around other people. Unfortunately, because of your belief that you cannot handle being in a relationship, you hold yourself back.

You deny your need for company and opt instead to be single. But this may eventually make you bitter and resentful of your gift. Believing that you are not built for romantic love limits your ability and your quality of life.

You may choose not to nurture your gift because you see it as the reason you cannot have the same happiness that you sense in others. You feel cheated and decide to shut everything out.

However, this is a belief that you need to overcome. Highly sensitive people like you can have successful and lasting relationships. You just need to manage it in a different way. Your abilities do make it more challenging but certainly possible. And just like with non-empaths, it all starts with finding a partner who can understand and accept you just the way you are.

Setting boundaries will be extremely helpful. The shield that you put up to protect yourself from the energy emanating around you will be beneficial for you and your partner. It can give you both peace of mind that his or her emotions and feelings are not influencing your own. There are other methods that you can learn to have a healthy relationship with your partner and still be able to grow as an empath.

11 - The Belief that Empaths are Emotionally Imbalanced

You know that there is absolutely nothing ordinary about what you can do. You have the ability to sense what others are feeling. Your gift has numerous benefits but sadly you find yourself reluctant to accept it. This is because you've been told that empathic abilities mean that you are emotionally imbalanced. You hear this perception from folks around you that you have started believing it yourself.

But the people who came up with this assumption on the mental state of empaths don't really have first-hand knowledge of what it feels to have your ability. To them, it just seems like you swing from one mood to another without any triggers.

They see you happy one minute and then angry or sad the next. There seems to be no reason for your rapid shift in emotions. They cannot understand your emotions and behaviors.

Your seemingly inexplicable reactions to what you see around you defy logic for them. Why are you intensely affected by a TV show or a movie? Why do you have difficulty watching the news? Why is it that it takes you a long time to get over what you see?

To non-Empaths, you do appear emotionally unstable. There is no other explanation for how you act. It is a fact that they believe to be true. Their firm belief that you are imbalanced is the same reason you acquire the same conviction.

When you are around these people, you sense that they are telling the truth about how they perceive you as an individual. You can also feel their fear and reluctance to spend time with you. And because of this, you start questioning yourself. Could it be that your abilities are making you emotionally unstable? That is the explanation that you give yourself for all the tumultuous emotions that rage inside you.

However, despite how true it may seem to them, you are not emotionally unstable. Your gift means that you are more in tune with the energy exuded by everything you are surrounded by. As an empath, you are dictated by your heart rather than your head. This makes it more difficult for you to stop yourself from being influenced by the emotions of others.

You drown in the huge amount of emotional baggage that

people both intentionally and unintentionally dump on you. As a result, you have an increased tendency of becoming depressed and anxious. You suffer from panic attacks that are caused by the combination of the emotions you pick up and your own inability to protect yourself.

Your mood swings and depression does not mean that you are emotionally imbalanced. You get these because of the way people around you feel. You are often not the source of the emotion you display but merely the conduit.

The belief that you are emotionally unstable limits the quality of life you lead. You retreat from other people and choose to be a recluse. This can be torture for an empath as you are naturally drawn to other people. Your craving to connect with others goes unfulfilled because you fear that your gift makes you emotionally incapable of handling interpersonal relationships.

12 - The Belief that Empaths become Addicts

Ever since you were little, you'd always struggled to handle the energy that you sense around other people. It was hard to reconcile why you felt certain things where there was absolutely no reason for you to feel it. For example, you wake up early and get a really great breakfast.

You listen to happy songs and find yourself singing along. You are in a good mood as you step out the door. But everything suddenly changes the minute you turn around and wave to your next-door neighbor.

She smiles and waves back at you. But then you start feeling anxious. You feel like something bad is going to happen. But when you think about what's going on in your life, you don't see anything to be anxious about.

You look at your neighbor one more time and you see that she has now gone back to whatever it was that she had been doing. And now you see a worried look on her face. She looks up and sees you looking at her and that smile is back.

The anxiety that had started bothering you seconds earlier is hers. Beneath the happy and smiling expression that she puts out for the world to see, she is struggling with something. Now it feels like you are the one feeling anxious.

Then somebody else walks past walking their dog. Your anxiety suddenly shifts to elation. These seesaws of emotions happen to you every single day. This is why there are times when you are reluctant to leave the safety of your own home.

When emotions and thoughts of others bombard you, you tend to look for a way to deal with them. It is human nature to try to escape from things that are troubling you. Sadly, the things that can give you momentary relief are not always healthy for you. You find yourself eating to comfort yourself.

When you feel extremely sad, you may binge on food such as chocolates or chips to make yourself feel better. Overeating may lead to health conditions such as obesity, diabetes, and heart ailments. In an attempt to overcome the emotions, you endanger your health.

There are even empaths who turn to even more dangerous habits. Alcohol and drugs become the only release from the surge of energy that they feel. Unfortunately, the more they turn to these 'comforts' the higher the fix they'll need next time. Being intoxicated or high poses a serious threat to the psychological and physical well-being of the empath.

Empaths are destined to become addicts. Substance abuse is the only way for you to have any sort of control over your life. You have heard this from other well-meaning folks who try to help you deal with your challenges.

This belief terrifies you. It makes you resent your gift. You become angry about the fact that your ability to sense and feel what others feel is ruining your life. Often, you'd end up forcing yourself to shut everybody out.

You refuse to develop your abilities because you are certain that it will just cause you more trouble. If you become a more powerful empath, then the compulsion for addiction will also increase. Unfortunately, the opposite is actually true. The less control you have over your abilities, the bigger the possibility that you will be driven to find other ways to deal.

Whether you choose to embrace your gift to help others or live a life protected from the turmoil of emotions of the rest of the world, the secret is in learning the right tools. Being an empath does not mean that you are destined to succumb to bad habits.

You still have the choice on how to deal with your abilities. Believing that addiction is inevitable holds you back from leading a productive life. Becoming an addict is a result of the choices that you make. It is not something that you are fated to become.

13 - The Belief that Empaths are Psychologically Frail

As an empath, you have the ability to sense what other people are feeling. And when you do, you take on that emotion as though it were your own. The result is that you shift from one emotion to another at the drop of a hat. While other Highly Sensitive People can understand what you're going through, most non-empaths just assume that you are moody.

Another thing that you are susceptible to because of your gift is your amplified reactions to what you witness. For example, you can immediately get profoundly emotional when you turn on the TC and watch the news. You see and feel the pain of the world so intensely that it physically affects you.

You see someone get beaten up, you feel like you're the one getting hit. You see news of famine on the other side of the world and you get immensely depressed at the sorry state of the world. This all makes sense to you. You know you are an Empath so you are aware of why you have such strong reactions.

Unfortunately, not everyone around you is accepting of your gift. You may have a few friends who understand what being an Empath means. This is despite them not having the same ability that you do. But to the rest of the world, your reactions are symptoms of something else entirely.

Abrupt mood changes, depression, and the lack of interest in interpersonal relationships are symptoms of mental health disorders. Folks around you begin suspecting that you are bipolar, schizophrenic, or clinically depressed. This is what most people will see. Sadly, they start treating you as somebody with psychological problems.

You get unfavorable reactions from the people you are trying to help. When you reach out and you tell them that you feel their innermost emotions, they lash out to protect themselves. Instead of admitting to themselves that Empathic abilities do exist, they conclude that you have an exaggerated sense of self-worth.

When you shift moods as a reaction to what you pick up, people tend to tell you to get help. Your abilities are not considered legitimate but are instead treated as some sort of ailment.

It is also unfortunate that their belief that you are mentally unstable has a huge effect on you. If you have embraced your gift, then being thought of as 'crazy' doesn't really give you much chance to help others. If you have not come to terms with what you can do, then you may just retreat even further from the outside world out of fear. Either way, you are held back by this myth about empaths.

You are perceived as weak minded and frail because of how you emotionally and physically react to the energy that you pick up from others. The inner turmoil caused by the barrage of emotions can at times be too overwhelming that you are unable to control how it affects you. As a result, people start noticing your actions and conclude that these are signs of a mental disorder.

However, despite this common belief of others, empaths are not psychologically frail. A testament to the mental health of Highly Sensitive People is that fact that their gift does not drive them to become clinically insane.

You need to be able to accept that your Empathic abilities are not going to be embraced by everyone around you. But this does not mean that you should accept their idea and consider yourself as psychologically fragile.

14 - The Belief that Empaths who are Unable to Repel Negativity are Weak

The reluctance to accept your gift isn't the only thing that holds you back from leading a healthy life or from being able to help others. Often, it is the perception that you are no good enough to be an Empath that affects you.

You understand that you have abilities that very few others do. But you question whether you deserve the extraordinary sensitivity that you have been born with. This self-doubt can be quite debilitating. But where does this self-doubt come from?

When you had finally come to terms with being an empath, you took the time to learn the tools to keep yourself protected. One of these tools is the ability to shield yourself from the negative energy around you.

Shielding is a very basic visualization tool that keeps you safe from the emotions and feelings that come from others. What you do is imagine yourself enveloped by other a bubble of light or surrounded by a wall so you can keep your energy in and the energy of others out.

Another tool that you learned was meditation. You took the time to enhance your own positive energy so you don't fall ill or get influenced by the negativity of others. Meditation was also a means to recharge yourself so you are better equipped to handle the turmoil of emotions that you encounter every single day.

Unfortunately, despite all your hard work, you still get affected by negative energy. You still feel drained after being around people who are in a bad mood or are feeling anxious. You still pick up and live through the emotions that result in negative actions such as being enraged or feeling inexplicably depressed.

When this happens, you start questioning whether you deserve to be an empath. Why is it that the tools that are supposed to help highly sensitive people are not working for you? Much of the self-help information that you have gathered showed that empaths are successfully able to live normal lives free from negativity with the same tools that you have been using.

So, why is it that you continue to absorb negative energy? Could it be that you are not a good empath? This belief starts to corrupt you and you end up with negative energy of your own. Your failure to repel negativity becomes a proof that you are weak.

Sadly, this belief limits you from being able to use your abilities to its full potential. You shy away from interactions where you would be exposed to other people. You believe that you are useless in helping others because you can't even help yourself. You lose faith in the methods that you are using as protection and end up leaving yourself even more exposed.

The tools that you learn to protect yourself are extremely useful. However, these do not guarantee that you will never pick up negative energy ever again. You are not weak. There are just different levels of negativity and different situations when you encounter them.

There will be times like when you're tired that you may not successfully repel what you want to keep out. But again, it does not mean that you are weak or that you are doing things wrong. It's very much like carrying an umbrella when it's raining. You still get wet a little bit, but the good news is that it keeps most of the rain away.

Negative energy is something that you will always be exposed to. There may be times that you won't be able to successfully keep it all out. But this definitely has nothing to do with any weakness on your part. As soon as you let go of the belief that it is your fault why you still get affected, the better your chances are of protecting yourself from negativity.

15 - The Belief that Empaths Cannot Function in the Workplace

A typical workplace environment is filled with stressors. There are deliverables that need to be completed and co-workers that one would need to adjust to. With so many things going on, there's guaranteed to be a huge amount of energy emanating from work. There are bosses who are stressing over operations.

They are constantly anxious about the performance of their employees and the profit that the company is making. Then there are the employees who go through a variety of emotions from worry to elation.

As an empath, you are sure to pick up the energy at your workplace. You come into the office and immediately get overwhelmed by the barrage of emotions. One of your co-workers may be feeling anxious over a missed deadline while another is feeling excited because of a recently completed task.

As a highly sensitive person, you will inexplicably be alternating between those two emotions. You will appear to be moody to everyone else. These shifts in moods may eventually affect your performance and the performance of the folks around you.

A lot of people believe that there's no room for emotions at work. This is why folks put up masks at the office. They exude an air of confidence even if they really are feeling insecure about their ability to do the job.

When someone gets promoted, co-workers fall over each other to congratulate the lucky person. They shower him or her with compliments and about how the promotion was well deserved. But most of these folks may not be as happy as they're projecting. They may be feeling resentful and even jealous.

Your ability to sense these hidden feelings can cause havoc with your own emotions. You see what other people are projecting but can tell that these are not the entire truth. You also start feeling what they are going through and this causes you a lot of confusion.

This is why quite a few Empaths choose to work isolated jobs. They find that not being in contact with the public helps them to focus better. However, this restricts the life of an empath.

Contrary to popular belief that Highly Sensitive People are loners, you actually crave to connect with others. Limiting your contact with the outside world may save you from picking up the emotions of other people but it has an adverse effect on you as an individual.

You end up feeling lonely and quite resentful of your abilities. You blame your forced isolation on your gift. And all this stemmed from the belief that as an Empath you are not equipped to handle a typical workplace environment. Unlike non-Empaths, your emotional and psychological makeup is not programmed for highly stressful situations.

The irony of this idea is that it isn't the job or the situation that you have difficulty with. It is the way other folks around you react to the stressors at the workplace that is challenging. But because of this common misconception of your capacity to adjust, you limit yourself from achieving your full potential as an Empath and as a professional.

The great news is that this is a myth. While it is true that you may find it difficult to do your job with the intense sea of emotions that you are exposed to, there are methods that you can learn to manage better. From visualization to meditation, the only limit that you have as an Empath is your will to try.

16 - Breaking Free of Limiting Beliefs

Your life as an Empath doesn't have to center around your abilities. There are various methods that you can use to keep the balance between your Empathic abilities and the rest of your life.

Limiting beliefs that are based on the perception of other people and your fears hold you back from realizing your full potential. Whether you choose to embrace the life of an Empath or just looking for a way to deal, below are some tools that can help you out.

Self-Awareness

Every single minute that you are exposed to the world, whether it's by spending time with others or even by simply turning on the TV, you open yourself to the energy around you. Emotions from other people overwhelm you and it can sometimes be terribly confusing. You can't tell half the time, whether what you're feeling is truly yours and not coming from somebody else.

The first step in coming to terms with all of the foreign energy is to take a self-inventory or self-assessment before any interaction. Think about what it is that you truly feel. Are you happy, mad, or sad?

What are the triggers in your life that are causing these feelings? Knowing which emotions are yours will help you with what you will be opening yourself up to. The other tools that you will be using to protect yourself need this basic step as a foundation.

You can keep a journal to keep track of what you're feeling. This is a great way to get started with getting to know yourself better. Jotting down what you really feel will give you a starting point that you can use as a way to keep all the emotions that will be surging through you in order.

For example, if you write down that you started the day happy and you get to work and suddenly feel anxious for no reason at all, then you'll be able to deal with it better.

Shielding

Shielding is a type of visualization that you can use to protect yourself. Once you're aware of which emotions are yours and which are not, you can work on separating them. Shielding will certainly help you to do that.

The first step in shielding is to visualize yourself surrounded by a wall. Some Empaths choose to picture themselves protected by a bubble of light. You can visualize any form of protection, from a raincoat or umbrella to a force field. This may seem silly at first. But the protection that you visualize must be something that you truly believe in. That will make it more solid and more powerful.

The shield will keep your energy separate from the ones emanating around you. You keep what is yours within your boundaries and you can keep the rest out. By doing that, you can minimize the effect that the emotions and feelings of other people may have on you. Picture it as oil and water. With the shield that you put up, you can keep the two separate.

Cleansing

Your ability goes beyond just being able to sense the energy around you. The emotions and feelings actually have an intense physical effect on you. You don't just relate to what other people feel, your empathic abilities mean that you actually feel what they feel. This can be quite overwhelming and exhausting. Cleansing is a great way to recharge your energy.

There are a lot of ways to cleanse yourself from all the foreign energy that you pick up. One of the methods is actually quite easy. The first step is to write down everything that you are feeling. You'll feel the urge to scream or cry or any other way to release the energy while you're writing everything down. There's no need to control any of these urges but it would be ideal to find a private place to do this at.

Once you have everything written down, burn the paper, and visualize all the emotions going away with the smoke. Doing this may not seem like a lot but it does help cleanse all the energy away. With your own energy recharged, you'll be able to function much better.

Another way of cleansing involves visualization. Just visualize a powerful beam of light shining all over your body. Visualize it going through every part of you and removing the energy from others bit by bit. It's like a shower or bath but something to wash away negativity instead.

Whichever cleansing method you choose, the important thing is that you do it on a regular basis. This will prevent the foreign emotions and feelings from building up and burdening you. You'll notice that after one of these rituals you feel a lot lighter and more relaxed.

Meditation

This method is a great way to recharge your energy. Some empaths who are not much into the spiritual aspect find themselves turned off by this tool. But meditation has nothing to do with religion or spirituality. This is a method that has huge benefits for you as an empath.

Meditation helps you be more in control of your thoughts. And since your thoughts are mainly the source of your dilemma, managing it will be very useful. The emotions that you pick up tend to cause havoc on your own, so keeping everything in control will be a huge plus. Your thoughts often keep you distracted. Thinking about the feelings and emotions helps you process what you are going through.

There are various types of meditation that you can try. The most basic one, of course, is finding a peaceful corner and clearing your mind. You don't necessarily have to sit on the floor in a lotus position. You can do it in any position that you find comfortable. You can even do it while taking a walk somewhere where you can relax. The point of meditation is to clear your mind.

This may not always be easy though. As soon as you try to start meditating, you'll find that everybody and their dog will be trying to connect with you. So, the first step is to find a place where there won't be much distraction. A secluded part of a park or your garden might be ideal for your meditation.

Another challenge that you'll be facing when you're meditating is that you'll find your head to be cluttered with a lot of things. From thinking about whether you left the stove on to what you'll have for dinner, there will be a lot of thoughts in your head.

When this happens, you'll need to take control. It may be a bit difficult at first so you would need to forcibly flush these thoughts out. Once you get used to your regular meditation sessions, you'll find that you'll have more control over your thoughts.

Setting Boundaries

You have the ability to sense energy from around you. But leaving yourself open to everything is not physically or mentally beneficial for you. As an empath, you are a natural healer, so you tend to take on responsibilities that are not yours. For example, if you sense that someone at your workplace is feeling anxious about their job, you naturally want to fix it. You may try to help out by doing their job for them.

Unfortunately, people around you will get used to unloading on you. You'll find yourself being asked to do things for others on a regular basis. Or you may also find yourself being the official confidant of the office. While these may seem like a great thing to do, it can get exhausting. This is the reason why you need to set boundaries.

While the shielding tool may help keep your energy separate from the rest of the world, it is still up to you on what you let in. So, make sure to limit the input to what you can manage. Choose carefully who to help and who to refuse. It is not your job to fix the entire world, so don't take on that responsibility.

Take a Bath

This may seem trivial, but taking a bath actually helps. It combines meditation and cleansing so you get two methods done at the same time. Placing herbs and essential oils in your bath water such as sage can help you relax better and make the experience even more pleasant.

So, whenever you begin feeling like you're about to be overcome by the tumultuous emotions raging inside you, take a 15-minute break and just soak in the tub. Lighting a few candles and playing relaxing music also goes a long way so you may want to get these set up as well.

Connecting with Others

Empaths may appear like loners to the rest of the world. But you know that the opposite is actually true. You crave companionship and friendship. And what better way to achieve this than by reaching out to other Empaths. There are often communities or organizations online that you can become a part of. However, you still need to take precaution to ensure that you pick the right people to connect with.

You can also spend time with non-Empaths such as friends or family that exude positive energy. These are the folks that you feel pleasant being around with. Since you pick up the emotions and feelings of those around you, it will be beneficial to hang out with folks that actually make you feel better.

17 - Conclusion

Being an empath is no easy thing. But having special abilities does not mean that you can no longer live a happy life.
Limiting beliefs hold you back from nurturing your gift and
having healthy interpersonal relationships. By fully understanding these beliefs and knowing the different tools that
you can use to protect yourself, you can improve the quality
of life that you lead.

Book 2 - A Plan For The Highly Sensitive

A Plan For The Highly Sensitive (Creative Genius, Dealing with Energy Vampires, Self-Defence, Building Relationships)

1 - Introduction

Being an Empath means you are sensitive to emotions. Basically, that is what empathy is about. However, it's possible that you may be receptive to more than feelings. When this is the case, you may be a Highly Sensitive Person as well.

Some people consider Empaths as the same with Highly Sensitive Persons. This is not the case. Although there are HSPs who are empaths, being an empath does not automatically mean that you are a highly sensitive person. It depends on how your nervous system functions.

Highly Sensitive Persons are those that have a sensitive nervous system. According to estimates, 15 to 20 percent of people have the condition. Having a nervous system that absorbs more stimuli doesn't make a person an Empath. It is said that only 2 to 3 percent of people are Empaths.

This book is for the Empath who is also highly sensitive. It will make you understand both conditions: being an Empath and being an HSP. It will guide you in dealing with your unique circumstances and help you make the most of what you are born with.

HSPs are rare, while HSPs who are also Empaths are even rarer. Thus, it is natural for people to misunderstand your unique traits. Understanding who you are will help you manage your unusual situation. Likewise, knowing about your condition will enable you to adjust your behavior to make it easier for others to connect with you.

But you must understand one thing: you are not sick. You are just wired differently. If you feel that there is something wrong with you, change your perspective of your situation. Your circumstances have made you choose the decisions you took before, whether they led to positive or negative outcomes. You can stop blaming yourself for things that were the result of your biology.

Studying about your circumstances will help you make better decisions. It is understandable that you will feel challenged right now, but be assured that you can do certain things that will help your life become easier and more fulfilling.

Remember that reading about these tips is different from applying them, and for real change to take place, you have to apply them regularly. Let us begin with knowing more about High Sensitivity – the trait that sets you apart from the rest of the majority.

2 - The HSP Empath Defined

HSPs and Empaths are known for their high sensitivity. They are unlike everybody else because they can feel more.

Society largely misunderstands this sensitivity. Some consider it as weakness, especially since the culture nowadays is to be tough and ruthless. Others see it as a disorder. The things that bother an HSP or an Empath are easily ignored by the rest of the population; the common assumption is there must be something "wrong" with them.

Regardless of this, the sensitivity of HSPs and Empaths make them stand out in a good way. They naturally do things that others rarely or never do. Although they have their flaws, they can excel at their tasks if they set their minds and hearts to it.

The amazing thing about them is that they often have troubled lives, but that does not stop them from caring about others – even if they are misunderstood or taken for granted. They do this because they can sense what others sense and feel what they feel. It is as if they are one with those around them.

Whether you are an HSP, or an Empath, or an HSP Empath, your sensitivity does not make you a weak person. It means that you are highly unusual with valuable gifts that must be used wisely.

What are the characteristics of HSPs?

Highly Sensitive Persons are those that are hypersensitive to stimuli (external and internal), have deeper cognitive processing, and high emotional reactivity. Their sensitivity is a result of the way their nervous system is constructed.

HSPs have higher sensitivity to the following internal and external stimuli:

- Sensory stimuli (sight, sound, smell, taste, and touch)

- Internal stimuli (pain, hunger, thirst, arousal, etc.)

- Emotions (their own and others')

- Subtle changes in other people and the surrounding

- Their own intuitions

3 - HSP characteristics are summarized with the acronym DOES

Depth of Processing

HSP's high sensitivity is sometimes called Sensory Perception Sensitivity. They process external and internal stimuli more thoroughly than usual because of their central nervous system's makeup.

Normally, information received by the brain gets processed through "filters" to make us become aware and understand what's going on inside and outside of our bodies. HSPs have more of these filters, thus they have greater awareness and insight than most people.

This depth of processing makes them capable of coming up with creative and unusual ideas. They are also more conscientious because they are acutely aware of the consequences of not doing a task well – thus, they can be perfectionists. Because they hate making mistakes, they tend to do things at a slow place, constantly checking for errors and correcting them as they go along.

The downside of this more thorough processing is that it consumes a lot their energy to process things. They tend to spend a lot of time considering the different possibilities, so they often delay making decisions. On the bright side, although HSPs can be indecisive, the choices they do take often tend to be right.

Overstimulated

HSPs are easily stressed by chaos, noise, working with other people, and working under a deadline. They prefer to be in quiet and serene places, doing things on their own or only with people they are most comfortable with. They often avoid social situations because they get drained by being with other people.

Emotionally Reactive

HSPs react strongly to emotion. They can develop intense feelings in response to both good and bad feedback. They are the quickest to show emotions, and they are likely to display emotional outbursts when others do not. They are more empathetic with other people even if they are not their family or friends.

They know more about their companions because people, in general, find it easy to talk with HSPs. They have keen observation skills (especially if the HSP is also an empath). They are concerned about how others will feel and they usually know what to do to make them feel better.

Sensitive to Subtle Stimuli

HSPs notice what most don't. This attention to details makes them more likely to adjust things in the environment to make it more comfortable for themselves and for others. They are the first to comment about small changes in other people and in the environment. They have detailed memories and can remember what others have a hard time recalling.

4 - High Sensitivity Is Not

High sensitivity is a fairly new term created by Dr. Elaine Aron, a clinical psychologist who studied the condition in depth and wrote about it in 1992. Because of this, many misconceptions about it still exist. To clarify this, Dr. Aron lists some things that HSP is not:

A Disorder

HSP is not a psychological disorder or a neurosis. A neurosis is a behavioral disorder without apparent cause, while HSP has a biological basis. An HSP breakdown may appear to be a neurosis only when people don't know that High Sensitivity causes it.

Shyness

Shyness is learned while HSP is inherited. HSP's initial hesitation to engage in social interactions or try new things can be mistaken as shyness, but they just prefer to process sensory data first before diving in.

Introversion

Introverts are more concerned with their inner, mental world than the external, physical world. They relish exploring their feelings and thoughts. They get energized by being alone and drained by being around people. Although about 70% of HSPs are Introverts, it does not follow that HSPs and Introversion are the same thing.

Why There Are Highly Sensitive People

Being an HSP is mostly inherited. Twins that were raised apart both had HSP behaviors. However, there are cases when only one of the twins developed the trait even if they are genetically identical to each other. This means that the trait is not entirely genetic.

Evolution favors traits that are beneficial in some way. Although being an HSP can be burdensome, it can provide a lot of benefits for you and perhaps the human species.

One advantage of being an HSP is that you can detect subtleties and changes in the environment that many often miss. This enables you to detect possible that other people don't immediately notice. You tend to consider more possibilities than most people.

Many will do things without thinking about the consequences, but as an HSP, you look at every angle and analyze them until you arrive at the most appropriate decision or action.

In a society, HSPs can become good advisers and caretakers. They serve as the counterbalance to impulsive individuals, making them stop before they make unwise decisions. They are also good in creating and innovating because they notice more things and reflect more deeply.

Circumstances can make the trait develop or disappear. Children who are stressed at home tend to become HSP. Trauma can also sensitize a person and turn him/her into an HSP.

When HSP children are forced to be less sensitive by their parents or by their circumstances (such as when they live in a busy and noisy place), they eventually become numb and less cautious. Likewise, repeatedly being exposed to a specific kind of stimuli can decrease someone's sensitivity to it.

It's both possible that you inherited your high sensitivity or you have developed it because of what happened to you. If you were highly sensitive when you were a baby, then it's more likely that you were born with the trait.

Signs of Being an HSP

Are you easily overwhelmed by sensory input? As an HSP, you will be greatly affected by stimuli around and within you. Bright lights, loud noises, coarse textures, and strong smells bother you. There are certain things that don't bother others but they annoy you a lot, such as the sound of the air-con or a leaking faucet.

Since your brain registers more of what you sense, you appreciate delicate sights, sounds, tastes, and sensations more than others can. This can make you love music, the arts, and good food. Sometimes you may get emotional because of them.

You perceive distinctions more clearly. Thus, you can spot mistakes faster. You know what needs to be done to correct something or to make it better.

You tend to be greatly affected by other people's feelings. This is common among HSPs but if you're also an Empath, you are likely aware what another person is feeling even if they don't show it. There are times when Empaths know what another person is going through even if he/she is far away. This is an example of extra-sensory perception –

something that distinguishes Empaths from HSPs.

Having a sensitive nervous system makes you become more reactive to many different things. You may develop allergies to medication, food, and substances. Small amounts of caffeine can make you palpitate. Sugar can make you feel ill. Your skin may become prone to rashes and itching. Sometimes, the full moon may even cause you to feel weird.

Your hypersensitivity causes you to be more cautious. You prefer sticking to what you're used to and you are likely to reject changes. Big life changes may unsettle you a lot that you get panic attacks. Your reactions can stress you out, more than the situation at hand.

When forced to try something unusual, you prefer studying it until you get used to it. You may spend a long time thinking about things until it paralyzes you. This may have caused you to miss some opportunities in the past.

Because you get burned out easily, you dislike having a packed schedule. You perform poorly when find yourself competing with others or if you are being watched. However, you can produce excellent output when you work by yourself at an unhurried pace, especially because you can focus deeply when you're not distracted.

Other people's effect on you may cause you to become a loner. When you are stressed, you often recharge by seeking solitude. You like places where you can be alone in peace, such as in a dark and quiet room.

You often turn your attention inwards when your surroundings overwhelm you. Because of this, you have an interesting inner life. You also know yourself well and can think quite deeply. You tend to analyze what you think and feel all the time.

Your inner focus and your avoidance of stimuli may cause you to be perceived as shy and unfriendly. However, this may not the case – you are not shy, you care about others, but you get easily drained by other people's actions and behaviors, that you tend to shy away from them.

There may be instances when you suddenly burst out emotionally. This may have caused others to tell you to stop being a baby or to not take things too personally. Now that you know that it has something to do with your physical attributes, you don't have to feel guilty about being "onion-skinned".

Because you are perceptive, you are conscious of what other people think about you. You don't want to upset them because you feel others' emotions quite easily especially if you're an empath as well. The sad result of this is that you may have been taken advantage of a lot of times.

Since you have more awareness of things and people around you, you tend to care more too. You know whether someone is uncomfortable and you go out of your way to make them feel better.

Seeing people in distress makes you uncomfortable, even when they are just acting. This is why you shun violent TV shows. When you watch dramas, it's easy for you to cry along with the characters.

Despite all these hassles, your unique brain and nervous system make you wiser than usual. You are more aware of things that you have a pretty accurate intuition about them.

Having an active brain makes you consider the past and future more. Thus, you know why things are how they are now, and you can foresee how they may turn out. This increases your analytical skills, making you seem psychic to other people.

Your hardworking brain makes you learn without being aware of it. You can synthesize knowledge and information in creative ways. You may even surprise yourself because you are likely to know things that you don't remember learning.

Your creativity and attention to detail can turn you into a highly skilled artist, inventor, or visionary. This will be natural for you especially because HSPs develop a love for fine things.

These are a few other things that HSPs are known for:

- HSPs are easily aroused by new or intense stimuli than most people.

- Having a sensitive nervous system doesn't mean that they have sharper senses, their brains just registers more data.

- Their brains filter out less information and take in more.

- They tend to process things more.

- They tend to reflect more on a lot of things.

- They sort things more precisely.

- They recover more slowly from strong stimuli.

Remember the acronym DOES so that you can spot an HSP more easily. Knowing who the HSPs are around you will help you feel less alone.

What are Empaths?

Empaths have the paranormal ability to know other individuals' emotional states. When speaking about empaths, people usually refer to those people who can tune into other humans' feelings, but there are those who can connect with plants, animals, and even nature.

Empaths can be quite popular in a group because they always seem to say the right things about other people. They are generally nice people who don't usually lie and who can tell whether somebody is lying. The more intuitive ones often become professional psychics. If you know a tarot reader or a psychic consultant, ask if he/she is also an Empath like you – there's a big chance that he/she will say yes.

Why There Are Empaths

Empaths are psychics that are attuned to emotions. As of now, it is still uncertain why some people become psychics. Some say that psychic abilities are natural consequences of having a soul which transcends the limitations of time and space.

These abilities don't manifest for everyone because not everyone is in touch with their spiritual nature. Others say that the nervous system has something to do with these gifts.

There are theories about how empaths are able to pick up emotions and information. Empaths may be able to perceive energy from the environment. They may unknowingly create energetic cords to those around them.

Empaths are said to have permeable boundaries that allow them to absorb and process more input. In comparison, non-empaths have stronger barriers that cause them to focus more on themselves. This barrier may be psychological but some say that this exists as an energy shield. This sensitivity makes them similar to the HSPs.

Like high-sensitivity, psychic ability seems to be genetic because it runs in certain family lineages. People may also become psychics and empaths because of circumstances or if they undergo psychic development training.

5 - Signs of Being an Empath

Here are some questions that will help you know whether you are an empath or not. The more Yes answers you have, the more likely that you are one:

- Do you feel other people's pain as if it was your own?

- Can you sense what other people mean even if they're saying something else?

- Do you get exhausted when being with others for a long time?

- Do you associate certain feelings, thoughts, or sensations to a specific individual consistently?

- Does the presence of some individuals make you feel ill?

- Does your mood change depending on who you're with?

- Do you get overwhelmed when you are caught in the middle of a group of people in a room or area?

- Do your emotions confuse you?

- Does your mood change without you knowing why?

- When spending time with someone, do you notice that you start acting like him/her?

- Do people go to you to talk about their problems?

- Do they share a lot about themselves to you?

- Do you prefer being in nature than in the city?

- Do you feel sick when you watch violent shows?

- Do you believe that animals and plants have consciousness and feelings?

- Do you find yourself attending to the needs of others more than your own?

- Do you notice energy in your body or around you?

- Do you cry easily?

- Are you careful of what words to say to avoid upsetting people?

- Can you tell what a person is feeling even if they try to hide it?

- Do you find it hard to distinguish your own feelings from others?

- Do you have accurate impressions of people, events, objects, places, etc?

- Can you easily tell if somebody is lying?

Empaths share many traits with HSPs. The important difference is that empaths are more attuned to the emotions of others, sometimes unexplainably so. The next section will discuss more of these differences.

Differentiating HSPs and Empaths

HSPs and Empaths are frequently considered as the same because they are both sensitive, but they are actually different in certain aspects.

Empaths are psychic. They know what other people feel not by merely watching their body language or imagining how they will respond given their conditions, but by using ESP (extra-sensory perception).

Sometimes, they may also have other psychic abilities such as clairvoyance (seeing spirits and energy), psychometry (retrieving information by touching an object), and telepathy (knowing what other people think). This is what makes them different from other people who can "empathize".

An empath knows the emotional state of another by feeling it himself/herself or by having an intuition about it. A sign that a person is a true empath is when he/she is accurate about what another feels most of the time (if not all the time). He/she will be correct even if the person is in a different location and undergoing circumstances not known to the empath.

HSPs are those with a nervous system that processes more information than the average person. They can pick up on tiny nuances that escape most people, thus they can appear psychic. Like empaths, they may be good at reading people, but unlike them, they rely on their normal senses to do so.

As mentioned, Empaths are rarer than HSPs. Many Empaths are HSPs, but only some HSPs are Empaths. A person can be an Empath and not an HSP, and vice versa. One condition does not necessarily lead to another, but there are many overlaps between their traits.

Pros and Cons of being an HSP and Empath

As mentioned, being an HSP is advantageous because you notice more things and you are able to think more thoroughly. This means you are quick to spot errors and dangers – and you can use this skill to help yourself and other people.

Because you are highly sensitive, you feel things intensely, thus, you can empathize with other people. You are a good listener and can give excellent advice. This makes you conscientious, responsible, and caring. You can help in ways that are not possible for many people. When someone needs help, you are often the first one to help.

You experience the world more than the average person. You see colors more vividly, hear distinct sounds, and detect subtle tastes in food. This can turn you into a great artist, musician, or chef.

Being both an HSP and an empath means you can be accurate with making evaluations. This makes you a good problem solver not only with things but with relationships as well.

Your thorough perception of people means you know who to trust and who to stay away from. You can connect with others more deeply since you understand them more, thus you can potentially influence them easily.

The disadvantage of high sensitivity is that you are easily frazzled and overwhelmed by things that don't normally bother the average person. It doesn't take much for you to get surprised. You are extremely bothered by bright lights and noise. You are quick to internalize emotions and empathize with other people's feelings, which may cause you to suffer.

It may be hard for you to enjoy movies, shows, and the like with friends when these portray people who are suffering. You are aware that they are not real but you still feel for them.

Your kindness may lead people to take advantage of you. Because you don't like to cause pain (because you can feel it, too), you may find yourself not fighting back when you should. You may have missed opportunities because you let other people have it. You may also spend more of your resources (energy, time, and money) for others rather than yourself, causing you to become depleted quickly.

Although you can be quite insightful, your perceptiveness may stand in the way of your objectivity. Because you reflect too much, you may have problems deciding. Making hard decisions that impact others negatively can be difficult for you.

Empathizing too much can make you feel as conflicted and powerless as those you are giving help too. This can paralyze you, which will frustrate you and the other party even more.

Picking up both sensory stimuli and emotions to a great degree can overwhelm you quite rapidly. This can be stressful and can take a toll on your health.

Seeking relief from sensory and emotional overload may cause you to avoid people and certain activities. Those you are with may not understand this. They might think that you are being mean to them or that something is wrong with you.

There are both good sides and both sides to being who you are. The secret to living a happy life is to work around your weakness and make the most of your strengths.

HSP Brainwaves

A study led by Carolyn Robertson revealed that HSPs have brainwaves that are mostly in the theta state. In comparison, the average person is often in beta.

The theta state is similar to a trance. It causes daydreams and creative ideas to enter into one's awareness. A person goes into this state when he/she is relaxed and not doing anything. This is a receptive state and naturally occurs when attention is directed inwards.

Because theta is HSP's normal level of functioning, they get easily overwhelmed when they have to process stimuli. Their awareness is larger than most people's and their nervous system filters less input than normal. When HSPs' attention is directed externally, they process stimulation more thoroughly than normal so they become overloaded easily.

People who have been practicing meditation for a long time can be in theta but they are still able to block out data because they've learned to control their focus. Similarly, HSPs must learn how to direct their attention away from things that they don't want or need to notice. They must find ways to protect themselves from unpleasant stimuli.

The succeeding chapters in this book will give more useful techniques for you to be more comfortable as an HSP Empath. This book also has an entire chapter dedicated to the practice of meditation.

6 - Coping Techniques for the HSP Empath

Having the unique biology and psychology of an HSP Empath can be a blessing or a curse depending on how you deal with them. Although you may be burdened by things that most people won't have to go through, you don't need to despair because there are a lot of ways for you to cope.

Health

Being an HSP requires you to take extra care of your health. If you haven't done so yet, note down what causes you to become ill. Make sure that you take measures in avoiding them.

Before eating something, know whether it contains an ingredient that you're allergic to. Keep anti-allergic medication handy.

You don't have to tolerate medication that causes uncomfortable side-effects. Tell your doctor or pharmacist that you are experiencing allergic reactions to the medicine he/she has prescribed so he/she can give you something else.

Do mild exercises regularly. If you're sitting for prolonged periods of time, get up and do stretches every 15 minutes. Walk outside so you can get fresh air.

Keep yourself healthy by consistently practicing good health habits and staying away from things that make you ill. This will greatly enhance your quality of life despite having a sensitive body.

Food and Drink

Being an HSP Empath makes you doubly sensitive to the things you consume. Not only will your nervous system react to substances it is not used to, but you will also respond to its energetic qualities. Select what you eat and drink carefully. Eat nourishing meals unhurriedly.

Some recommend being vegan to avoid the negative energies of slaughtered animals. Reduce your consumption of unhealthy food. If you can't stay away from food which is not good for you (physically or energetically), bless your food.

Drink plenty of clean water to hydrate and purify your body. Avoid drinking too cold or too hot drinks though, as this may be intense for your nervous system.

Environment

Keep yourself healthy by maintaining a clean surrounding. Make this a routine. The effort you spend will be well worth your added productivity.

Get rid of harmful fumes in your home and office. Hire a reliable air quality service for it. Have air filters cleaned regularly.

Clean your place at least once a week. If you're allergic to dust, hire a cleaning service. Wear a face mask if you want to do the cleaning yourself. Use gentle cleaning products and adequate protection.

Since disorganization affects your nervous system negatively, get rid of your clutter. Arrange your items and furniture so everything is neat and in its proper place. Make it easy to live/rest/work/play in that place.

Are you sensitive to electromagnetic frequencies? EMF can cause symptoms like uncomfortable sensations, ill health, and psychological difficulties. The main sources of EMF are anything electric (electrical outlets, appliances, gadgets), cellphones, cellphone towers, cordless phones, wireless routers, power lines, and metal plumbing.

Use an EMF meter to check how much you are exposed to. There are ways to reduce the level of EMF in your area so you don't have to move out just yet.

If you're also sensitive to subtle energy, consider following Feng shui guidelines in modifying your area. Not only will this be aesthetically pleasing, it may enhance your well-being, too.

Other People

Pay less attention to what you are feeling inside and more to what's going on around you. This will help take your mind off excessive stimulation during social interactions. Be curious about others instead of focusing on the things that might go wrong.

Compromise with other people on things you have no control over and let them take over. Be polite when requesting others to make some changes so that you will feel less frazzled. Don't hate people who enjoy more stimuli than you. Make them understand how their actions are affecting you.

Desensitize yourself by letting yourself mingle. Do not think too much; just meet people and talk to them. You will discover that hesitating only makes interacting with them harder.

There are so many things you can learn from and teach to other people. Don't let your nerves get in the way of that. You can always regain whatever energy you feel was drained from you. This is just a normal part of high sensitivity; it does not mean you should shun social activities forever.

Don't expect too much from others. Expecting something to happen and it doesn't materialize can be disappointing. If you demand other people to be considerate towards you, the same way you are considerate of them, and they don't oblige may cause you extreme disappointment and frustration.

On the contrary, when you're nice just because you're that way, and you know that other people may or may not be nice in return, then you spare yourself the hurt of being disappointed.

Before you do anything, ask yourself: do you want this for yourself or do you think others will appreciate your kind gesture and return it? It's best if you depend on your own self to be happy.

Talk with Someone Who Understands

Observe the people around you – some of them are HSPs and empaths like you. Talking with them can help you feel less out of place. Share coping tips. If you can't find someone like you, reach out to a caring counselor or psychiatrist.

Stimulation

Manage how much stimulation you expose yourself to. Balance your level of stimulation. Don't get too much so you won't feel anxious or too little to cause you to be bored.

Determine objectively and realistically the times when you must push yourself to face stimulation and when to avoid it. Change what you can and don't be too worked up by those that you can't do anything about.

Limit watching TV. You may not notice it yet, but watching certain shows may stress you out. Also, studies say that spending less time in front of a TV will lengthen your life. Use your TV time exercising instead. If you still need to watch TV, mute commercials. These are usually louder than the show you're watching.

Bring headphones or earplugs and use them when you find yourself in noisy environments. Install soundproofing in your rooms if you must. If not, you can use white noise, relaxing music (without lyrics), or noise-cancellation devices. Spend time doing quiet activities to help de-stress.

Paint your room in calm colors like green, blue, and white. Bright colors like red, yellow and orange may be too bright for you. Remove anything that hurts your eyes.

Adjust lighting when you can. Wear dark eyeglasses during sunny days. Avoid bright lights when it's dark outside.

Know how your senses react to different stimuli and prepare accordingly. This will help decrease your stress level immensely.

Routines

Create a routine of all your activities so it takes less than the amount of energy that you should exert doing them. Decisions cost energy. By minimizing choices and possibilities to consider, you can keep more of your energy.

Try to wake up at the same time every day to have a stable body clock. Avoid the temptation to wake up and sleep at random hours to avoid sleeplessness and fatigue, especially when you're about to do a lot of things the next day.

Set a morning routine that enables you to organize your entire day. Use the first few minutes to plan what you must do and when to do it. If you need to accomplish a task that requires brainpower, do it during the first three hours upon waking up when your mind is functioning at its peak.

Find something that uplifts you and do it as soon as you can, as often as you can. Writing about your thoughts and feelings will help you release negativities and at the same time process them.

If you have a morning routine, you should also have an evening routine. This should let you sleep comfortably. Make sure that your bed suits you and gives you a restful slumber. Change your bed if it's worn out already.

Before sleeping, review what happened during the day. You may think about them sequentially if that helps you recall them more clearly. Where you able to do what you have planned in the morning? How did you handle problems and challenges? What could you do to spend the day better next time? Sleep on this so you will have fresh ideas in the morning.

Time Management

Manage your activities so you'll have less stress. When you have a plan, you avoid having to select what to do among several possibilities.

Schedule challenging activities on off-hours so you won't have to wrestle with the crowd and noise while you do them.

Do not do too many things at one time. Scheduling will make you see what you need to do and know whether you are attempting to do too much. Give yourself enough time to do things at a comfortable pace.

Set aside time for you to recuperate. Include this in your schedule to ensure that you have the time to exclusively take care of yourself.

Reduce your obligations. Learn to say no if you notice that you are becoming overwhelmed with a lot of things. Never sacrifice your own comfort for the sake of pleasing others. Remember that the time you spend doing what you don't want is time that you'll never take back.

Traveling

Allocate time for commuting. Listen to calming music or turn off the radio. This will help you focus more and be less frustrated by the noise. Drive along the slow lane. Avoid rush hour traffic if you can.

Relaxing

Receive massages. Studies have shown that they decrease stress levels. They give you safe and tolerable stimulation. Give feedback to the therapist so that he/she can give you the appropriate amounts of pressure.

Taking warm baths during the cool weather (or cold showers during summer) can be refreshing. Swim. Water has therapeutic effects upon the body.

From time to time, indulge in things that relax you. Pamper yourself in a spa. Watch a beautiful sunset with your special someone. Bake a cake. Even if you think you have so many things to do, fit it in your schedule. This is important for HSPs.

Identify What Makes You Uncomfortable and Plan What to Do with Them

Are there certain things that cause you stress – being in crowded places or talking to a person you don't like, for instance? Take note of them and create action plans for dealing with them. Determining what to do beforehand makes it easier for you to avoid overthinking and just do what you have planned to do. Avoid stressors for as much as you could so you minimize the strain and burden to your nervous system.

In general, these are HSP's difficulties:

- Easily distracted by stimuli, noise, chaos, and conflicting interests

- Stresses out quite quickly

- Can't handle conflict well

- Not good in setting boundaries

- Focusing more on others' needs than your own

- Gets nervous when being watched

- Perfectionist

- Indecisive

- Feeling out of place

- Commonly misunderstood and judged harshly

- Acts slowly

- Thinks too much

- Gets hurt easily (physically and emotionally)

- Feels emotions strongly and can sometimes lash out, walk out, or break down in tears

- Reaching sensory overload more quickly than most people

- Needing more rest and sleep

What are the things you find challenging? Knowing them makes you cope better.

Look for Things that Energize You

Find things that make you feel empowered and put you in a good mood. Do you like spending time with your family? Do you feel good sitting under a tree? No matter what it is, do it as often as possible, especially at times when you are feeling drained.

Focus on Positive Things When You're Down

The things you focus on affect your mood, so if you're not feeling great, focus on things that uplift you. If you can't find anything positive around, remember the happy times. You can also focus on events that you are looking forward to.

Keep Yourself Busy

When you end up ruminating on something, switch to doing-mode to slow down your racing mind. When you are busy with something, your attention will be focused externally instead of internally, making you less likely to get locked in your own thought loops.

Just take care not to keep yourself too busy to the point of exhausting yourself. This might make you feel worse. You must pay attention to how you are so you will know whether something is good for you or not.

Stay in Nature

Being indoors in the city can cause an HSP empath to feel claustrophobic. It is said that emotional energy lingers in closed spaces. If you feel as if the energy of the place is not in harmony with your own energy, step out for a while.

Nature has a cleansing and invigorating upon the energy of the HSP Empath. It can have a stabilizing effect on those who feel out of place.

Have Kind Words for Yourself

Take note of the things you tell yourself. Are they kind or critical? If you don't like the way you are now, you will not change yourself by humiliating yourself. Pretend that you are saying to someone else the things you are saying to yourself in your own head. How would that person feel? If it's natural for you to be compassionate for others but not for yourself, try directing that gentleness towards yourself as well.

Coping with Indecisiveness

Indecision is one of the toughest challenges of HSPs and Empaths. These tips will help you overcome your inability to make quick choices.

Know What You Are Afraid Of

Being indecisive is a result of fear. Do not confuse worrying with problem-solving. Ask yourself, "What am I scared of? What is the worst scenario for this? If it did happen, then what? What could I do to handle the situation?" Clarify the fear. Understanding it will help reduce its effect.

Forget What You "Should" Do

Don't be sidetracked by what you think is expected of you. Indecisiveness may arise from trying to please different people. As a side-effect, you may subconsciously do the opposite of people's expectations to try to re-assert yourself. Thus, stop worrying too much about others' opinions. This will help clarify what you really must do.

Do Not Give in to Analysis Paralysis

Thinking too deeply may lead you having difficulty arriving at a decision. Don't assume that analyzing further will help you, especially if you're already stressed. If you can't decide, write the pros and cons of each option and give yourself a time limit – say, 5 minutes. Take a break and look at your list. Go with your first hunch.

Give Yourself Time

It's possible that you don't really have to decide right now. Take enough time to decide for as much as the situation permits. If you must think things through, ask for more time. This is to prevent being pushed into a decision.

Sleep on the decision. Take it off your awareness so your subconscious mind can work on it. You may receive insights about it later.

Pretend that You Have Already Decided

Trick yourself into deciding by pretending that you've already done so. This will put you in a positive mood which also clarifies perspective, allowing you to eventually make the appropriate choice.

Although you may not change much about how your mind normally works, you can become better at making decisions the more you take them. Take note of what helped you make a good decision. Don't be afraid to commit mistakes – everybody makes them from time to time.

Stay Away from Draining Situations

Recall the times when you felt drained. Some situations that may have cause you to feel depleted are the following:

- Feeling negative emotions – such as anger, sadness, fear, guilt, stress, helplessness, insecurity

- Being in places where you don't want to be

- Wanting to please someone

- Trying to fit in

- Helping someone at your own expense

- Being talked to excessively

- Harassment

- Acting unnaturally

- Lying/being lied to

- Being in abusive relationships

What can you do to avoid these situations? Plan for them. The more prepared you are, the better you will able to handle them when they happen.

Avoid People Who Drain You

Acknowledge people's effect on you. It may not go away just because you ignore it. There are certain kinds of people who will make you feel tired or weary when you interact with them. As an HSP who is also an empath, you are naturally more vulnerable to these types of individuals. Keep interactions to a minimum. Try not to be guilt-tripped into helping them.

Set Boundaries

As an empath, you need to work on your boundaries. You should be aware who you are and what are important in your life. Don't let people cross your boundaries even if you think you "should" let them.

You may be tempted to think that others need you. Don't think that you're doing others a favor by helping too much. There are those who are just taking advantage of you even if they don't really need your help. You must take care of yourself as well – your main responsibility and concern should your own well-being.

Even if you feel compelled to help people, protect yourself

so you don't wear yourself out. You must let them mature by letting them do things for themselves and own up to the consequences of their actions.

Like Yourself

You may be more sensitive to other people's opinions. Don't let negative impressions of you make you feel insecure, though. Having love for yourself will shield you from those who are not that kind to you.

Be Selective of Your Companions

Be with people you feel good with. Let go of those who deplete you in some way. Even if you are attached to some people, stay away from them for a while. This may make you become more objective about what their real effect on you is.

If people want to leave you, don't cling to them. Those who are on the same frequency as you will stick around while those who are not will naturally move away from you. Although it may cause unpleasant feelings, you will get over it.

Be More Expressive

Empaths are prone to absorbing feelings that they also keep what they feel. They don't want to upset others because that will be upsetting for them also. Separating yourself from other people will make you care for yourself more effectively. Be true to your heart and express what you feel. You need to speak up because most people aren't perceptive as you.

Problem Solving

These are some guidelines for problem-solving:

- Don't waste your time and energy on problems that can't be solved. Instead, shift your focus to where it's needed.

- Deal with one problem at a time. This will reduce the strain on your nervous system. It will make your head become clearer, allowing you to directly tackle the problem at hand.

- Don't overthink. Turn your attention to something else so your subconscious mind can get busy on it. The answer may come to you when you least expect it

– especially since your mind synthesizes the information it gathers in unexpected ways.

- Work on changing yourself and not on changing others. This will make things less frustrating for you. You will also be more productive when you dedicate your energy to yourself.

- Consider not doing anything for the meantime. Sometimes, you don't really have to do anything for the problem to go away. There are instances when you think you are in trouble but you realize that you're fine all along.

Remember that as an HSP, you are blessed with a sharp mind. You just need to learn how to keep stimuli in manageable levels to make it work efficiently.

7 - Managing Criticisms

Being an HSP you are more sensitive to criticisms, you are likely to take them personally. These are the things you can do to lessen the pain and benefit from negative feedback.

Refuse to be labeled

Accepting a label somebody has given you lets the other person dictate who you are. You are who you are no matter what people say.

If you're at fault, acknowledge it and apologize appropriately

If somebody says that you're late again and you really are, say, "Yes, I'm late, I'm sorry." This will let the other person know that you recognize your mistake and that you care about how they made them feel.

Ask for clarification

Criticism can be vague, which makes it hard to be used constructively. If you don't understand what the critic is saying, request that he/she be more specific. For example, you are told that you are being lazy. You can ask, "What makes you say that I'm lazy?" or "What should I work harder on?"

You may not control your feelings of getting but if somebody says something bad about you, the chapter on managing emotions will help you lessen the effect of negative emotion and recover fast.

Giving Complaints

Since you are an HSP and an Empath, you will be quite hesitant to say something that might offend another person. If you need to give a complaint, these steps will make it easier:

Name the problem

Say exactly what your problem is. Be specific, brief, and clear. Stick to the facts and avoid assuming things.

State your feelings

Say what you feel and what you think of the problem, as it is. Don't exaggerate. Don't even try to shame the other person, maintain the focus on yourself. Say, "I feel uncomfortable because of loud music", instead of, "You should be ashamed that you don't care about what others feel about your music."

Specify what you want

Say what you want directly. Don't beat around the bush, because you'll just become more frustrated when the other person doesn't get them. Avoid talking in riddles, thinking that the other person can interpret them.

Ask for reasonable changes one at a time so that others can manage to do it.

Remember that your mind tends to magnify emotions, so what you think will be devastating to others may not really matter to them at all. Try not to worry about others' feelings too much.

By now, you may have realized that there are a lot of things you can do to make life easier for you. But wait; what about handling emotions? Don't worry; there is a chapter for that.

8 - Keeping Emotions at a Manageable Level

Emotional management is controlling how you experience and express emotions. HSPs and Empaths feel emotions intensely, so this chapter will be useful for you. Following the tips given here will help you feel better and prevent you from going into an emotional outburst.

The most important thing you must do is learn to accept your emotions. They are part of you. Even if they seem to be too much for you at times, know that you can cope with them. Remember that your feelings are just temporary. You can do something about what you feel, maybe not now, but eventually, you will.

Meditate

You can meditate to help cope with being an HSP. Your emotions can serve as your meditation focus.

The goal of meditation is to focus your mind so that you stop being controlled by it. Accept your feelings as they are. While you are meditating, do not analyze, or try to change them. Observing emotions without resisting or embracing them will help dissolve them. Tell yourself that you are feeling the emotion but you are not the emotion.

Calm Down

Calming down reduces the stimulation of emotions and makes you more capable of thinking clearly. Taking deep breaths is an effective way to calm yourself. Relaxing tensed muscles is another.

These activities send a message to your brain that you are safe and that you are okay. Moving in a free and relaxed manner also tells your brain that you are not in danger and you can do what you want, so it will stop being agitated.

To further help your mind, switch your thoughts to relaxing ones. Recall peaceful moments or think about what you want to happen in the future.

Modify Your Perspective

Change your view about the situation. Your thoughts affect your emotions, so choose to think helpful, positive thoughts.

Focus On What's Important

We can't totally avoid unpleasant situations but we can control how we respond to them. Figure out whether the thing that's bothering you is worthy of your attention. The more energy you dedicate to unimportant things, the less energy you have for those that truly matter.

Fake It

The mind monitors your body and creates emotions based on its status. If you act as if you're experiencing certain feelings, your brain will think that you are really feeling them. The brain will cause physical changes that support that emotion. If you're sad, smile. If you're feeling afraid, act as if you're relaxed. It will eventually manifest in your actions and behaviors.

Process It

Thinking about what you feel will move your energy from feeling into thinking mode. Evaluate if your thoughts are helpful and true. If not, change them.

Express What You Feel

Emotions are bundles of energy that are designed to make you act. If you dislike what your emotions are telling you to do, let these emotions out of your system instead. You can do this through physical or artistic activities.

Enhance Positive Emotions

How many negative emotions can you think about? List those that you are prone to. Release them through the following ways:

- Leaving the cause of the emotion

- Being with those who give good feelings

- Physical movement

- Doing something you enjoy

- Being busy

- Visualizing emotions and pretending that they disappear or morphing into positive ones

- Reciting affirmations

- Expressing them

- Relaxing

- Observing feelings without holding on to them

- Meditating

- Naming the feeling

- Relabeling the emotion – example, fear into cautiousness, anger into energy, panic into excitement and so on.

- Knowing that the feeling will pass

- Being thankful of the good things you receive

- Using the emotion to do something beneficial

- Conversing with the emotion

- Analyzing the purpose of the emotion

- Focusing on the positive

Negative emotions prevent you from tapping into your inner resources. If you're feeling bad, your mind will be centered on things that strengthen those emotions. The stronger these feelings are, the worse you become.

Do this: go to a place where you can remain undisturbed for five minutes. Close your eyes. Recall a situation where you got stressed. What were your thoughts? How did they make you feel? Can you label the emotions? What physical effects did they give?

You may notice that you are now feeling what you felt back then. This is the power of your thoughts. What you think will influence what you feel. It doesn't matter if these thoughts are about something that happened long ago or something that never happened. For as long as you hold it in your mind, it will feel real, as if it's real.

Take a deep breath. Calm yourself. Clear your mind for about a minute, not thinking about anything. This time, imagine a positive experience. Observe the sensations that enter your awareness. How are they different from what you experienced in the previous exercise?

Always be vigilant about your feelings because they have a direct effect on your abilities. Be in control of your inner experiences by deciding what to think about. Controlling what goes on in your head will also control the way you respond to events. It strengthens your self-control, helps you think more clearly, and make better decisions.

One thought leads to other thoughts. It attracts connected and similar memories and concepts until you have a collection of them in your head. When this occurs repeatedly, a thought pattern is formed, and this may turn into a habit.

The brain conserves energy by creating shortcuts, thus this habit may be applied to situations even if doing so may not be helpful.

The mind looks for evidence to maintain a pattern of thought. It will also force consistency because keeping distinct emotions, thoughts, and reactions is difficult. Because of this, when you feel something, your perception is altered to confirm that what you are feeling is what you are thinking (or seeing). To overcome this, you must understand how you think.

Thinking starts with the brain selecting what you should focus on. Conscious awareness is limited so it will zero into what it thinks is important and relevant to your situation. It will then filter out the rest through the following ways:

- Deletion – discarding data

- Distortion – twisting the information to fit a central idea

- Generalization – broadening scopes to make them fit

a preconceived notion

These make thinking faster but may likely result to committing a lot of mistakes. Even if you are an HSP, you may still be prone to these shortcuts.

Remember that because of the limitations of human attention, perception, and thought, each of us has our own version of reality that is greatly different from objective reality. Two people may experience the same thing but will feel differently about the same experience, depending on his/her beliefs, attitudes, and past experiences.

Because your representation of reality is not perfect, be more willing to remake your beliefs and thoughts instead of treating them as the absolute truth.

When you become aware of an unpleasant emotion, find out what belief is making you react in a certain way. Challenge this thought. Must you really believe it? Are you better off with a different thought? How true is this? What will make this untrue? How can you think about the situation if you were a different person?

Changing your belief also changes your reactions.

Challenge your emotions. What is it trying to make you do? Do you really have to feel in that manner? What are the advantages and disadvantages of having this emotion? What else can you feel so that you can do things better? How can you deal with the underlying need for the emotion? Knowing the point of the emotion can enable you to act on it without being overwhelmed by what you feel.

Alter Your Memories

The way your memories are portrayed in your mind affects how you feel about them. Experiment with your memories.

Retrieve a nice memory. Describe the images. Are they clear or blurry? Do you see color? Are there predominant hues? Is it in entirely black and white? Do you see a frame around the memory? Is the scene like a picture or is it 3D? Do you see movement or is it still? Can you see yourself in the memory or are the events occurring around you?

Lessening the Effect of Negative Memories

Bring back an unpleasant memory. When you can see it in your mind, send it away from you until it disappears. Notice how doing this makes you feel. '

Changing Your Feelings

Upon eliminating the negative memory, immediately recall a positive one. Intensify it by making it more vivid and realistic. Bring the image closer to you and step inside it. Soak in the pleasant feelings.

Control your Inner Voice

Aside from choosing what words you say to yourself, you can also control the characteristics of your internal voice to change how you feel.

If you want to feel the desired emotion, think about what kind of voice will evoke it. If you want to be braver, hear the voice of someone whom you consider a hero. Talk to yourself with this voice. Talk about what you want to do. Say this repeatedly and increase the volume until you are convinced.

If you dislike what you hear from your internal dialogue, decrease it in volume until it fades to silence. You can also use a funny voice so you won't take it seriously.

By now, you may have realized that being an HSP/Empath is not so bad after all. It only takes some slight adjustments to what you normally do so that you can live your best life. There is a chapter that gives you another small but powerful tip: meditating regularly.

Meditation for the HSP Empath

Meditation can help increase your focus so you can eliminate negative stimuli and attend to certain tasks at hand. It can also help you manage your thoughts and feelings better so they don't overwhelm you. There are many meditation methods; those given here are only some of them. Explore different techniques until you find one or two that give you the best results.

To meditate, you must relax, focus on one specific thing, and return to it whenever you get distracted. You can meditate for as short as 5 minutes. To improve your skills though, try lengthening your sessions.

You may track the time you are meditating or not. If you decide to keep time, set a low-volume alarm for it so you won't be startled when it rings. You may stop the session when you want to.

To make meditation work, you must do at least 5 minutes a day. The best time to do it is in the morning when your mind is still free from too many thoughts of a busy work day. Choose one that works for you and stick with it for at least a month. You may struggle with this initially, but you will eventually notice several benefits that will inspire you to continue.

Reciting Affirmations

As you have read in the previous chapter, the thoughts you think about repeatedly becomes part of you. If you want to move towards a certain kind of reality, you must think about it constantly.

Affirmations are an example of repeated thoughts that are designed to create positive outcomes. Some examples of affirmations for HSP Empaths are the following:

- I accept that I am a Highly Sensitive Person. I take care of myself all the time.

- I feel other people's emotions but I remain calm and peaceful.

- I attract kind people and comfortable situations in my life.

- I am always protected.

- I let go of all emotions and energies that belong to others.

- I receive only the energy that is good for me.

- I only receive psychic information that I must learn and act upon.

- I am healthy in many levels.

- I appreciate who I am and others appreciate me.

These statements are said repeatedly and with conviction, preferably while you are in a suggestible state. A suggestible state is one that is receptive and non-judgmental such as when:

- You are deeply relaxed

- You are meditating

- You have just woken up

- You are about to sleep

You can make your own affirmations, but make sure that they meet the following criteria:

- You must believe they can happen.

- They are phrased as if they are happening already (phrasing it as something that is happening now will make it more convincing for your subconscious mind).

- They are easy to remember and repeat (keep them simple and short).

- They do not include negatives (if you used not or no, your mind will hear what it's negating – example: I will not feel anxious can cause you to be anxious).

Write down what you want more of and turn those into affirmations. Imagine what it would be like if it came true. Accompany your affirmations with visualizations of what you desire. This kind of meditation is easy to do and can be quite enjoyable.

Focusing on an Object

The goal of meditation is to hone your focus. Using an object and focusing on it is one of the most common techniques of meditation. You may choose anything you want for as long as you can hold your attention to it for a couple of minutes.

Adjust the lighting so that it's dim but bright enough for you to see the target. Place it at eye level at a comfortable distance from where you are sitting.

Keep gazing at the object without analyzing or judging it. Blink only when you need to. Avoid looking around or moving unnecessarily. If your attention wanders, set your eyes back to the target.

Focusing on an Idea

Meditating upon a concept makes you process and absorb it better. Close your eyes. Choose words that evoke desired state to you: serenity, harmony, competence, confidence, etc. You may create mental images to depict it. Imagine experiencing the state.

Mindfulness

Mindfulness meditation is one of the most popular techniques. It involves being closely aware of what's happening in the moment. You should do this without thinking about what you observe. Don't talk about it in your head. Just perceive it without thinking about it or explaining to yourself what's going on.

Keep your focus on the present moment. Resist the temptation to let your mind rummage your memories or go forward in time. When you notice a thought, you may say mentally, "Thought" and continue focusing. Let these drift into and out of your awareness. Your awareness must not get buried under a heap of thoughts.

If you notice something in your body, just feel it without doing anything about it as much as possible. Take note what it makes you feel, but keep still. Eventually, the sensation and the emotion will fade away.

You may do this outside of a meditation session. Judge less and observe more. Don't let old experiences block your current one. Attempt to perceive reality now, instead of what you remember it to be, or what you expect or wish it to be.

Beliefs limit perception. Let your thoughts rest to allow your awareness to roam freely. This will give you a fresh perspective, break free from mental patterns, and enable you to do more things.

Breathing Meditation

A lot of meditation techniques involve controlling the breath. As you have read earlier, deep breathing causes you to become calmer because doing so slows down your heart rate. On the other hand, if you want to be more energized, try breathing more quickly.

Pay attention to your breath at the exclusion of other thoughts. The more you do this, the better you can stop a flurry of thoughts from drowning you.

You may prolong your breath by counting the seconds that go by. Inhale through your nose while counting from 1 to 4. Let your belly rise as you do so – this is called diaphragmatic breathing and it is more efficient than regular breathing. Hold your breath and count 1 to 4 in your mind. Exhale through your nose. Exhale through your nose and count 1 to 8. Hold your breath for another 4 counts.

You may count as fast or as slow as is comfortable for you.

Repeat this for a couple of cycles.

Heartbeat Meditation

Being aware of your heartbeat will give you an idea of how your body responds to certain situations. Feel your pulse. Is it slow or fast? What is causing it to be that way? Try to change your breathing pattern and see its effect upon your pulse. You will have greater control over what you feel eventually.

You can also focus on your heartbeat if you are too distracted. Just pay attention to your pulse until you are no longer bothered by the things that are going on around you.

Sensing

You are sensing the world more fully so might as well use this to help your mind focus more. Sensing a target can enhance your mindfulness. Pick something that appeals to your senses. Explore it – how it looks like, how it feels like, etc. Do this for some time without talking about it in your head.

Music Meditation

Meditation may be done with music playing in the background, but it can be the focus of meditation itself. Listen to the music and let it carry you. Embrace the experience instead of separating yourself from the music by a torrent of ruminations.

Visualizing

Visualizing is another word for imagining. When you visualize, you train your mind into creating something – first mentally, then eventually, for real. Visualize your objectives, your aspirations, the things you believe in, or anything worthwhile to you.

Imagining something is also said to affect your energy. Thus, you may mentally create things that may help you cope with being an HSP empath. For example, you may visualize shields protecting you from harmful vibrations of the environment. You can also imagine unhealthy connections with other people as cords – cut them using tools forged by your imagination.

Facilitating Success

Whatever you focus on will affect you and your actions, so use meditation for something positive. If you have a problem, imagine going forward in time to the moment when it's already resolved. Experience with all your senses how it's like having solved the problem. Hold on to the positive feelings and bring them back with you to the present.

Even if you don't know how it will happen yet, just keep it in your mind. Focusing on a positive outcome makes you think more clearly – this helps you make better decisions that will eventually lead to desired results. What matters is that you create a mindset that will allow you to progress.

Writing

You can meditate as you write. Express your suppressed ideas and feelings and process them through writing. Communicate with whoever you want through paper even if you won't give it to them. Write freely and don't edit it – this allows your subconscious mind to surface. Release whatever's bothering you. Afterward, read and reflect on what you've written. This can help you see things with fresh eyes.

Progressive Relaxation

Progressively relaxing your muscles can relieve frazzled nerves and cause you to enter a better state of mind. You may begin with your toes and work up or start with our head going down.

For example, notice the top of your head. Do you have a headache? Imagine the headache dissipating. Stop wrinkling your forehead. Make your forehead as relaxed as you can get it. Feel the sensations on your face. Smile as wide as you can and let your jaw become limp.

Move your head from side to side, then forward and backward, until your neck becomes more relaxed. Raise your shoulders then let them fall back limply. Shake your arms. Open and close your hands a few times then put them on your lap. Continue tensing and releasing muscles this way until you reach your toes.

When you're done, spend a couple of minutes relishing how relaxed you are. Don't think of anything. Just experience it. Remember that you could always do this when you want.

Mental Relaxation

You can relax mentally if you release what's troubling you and refocus on your chosen target. You may also visualize things that cause you to relax deeply.

What brings you deeper into a passive state of mind? Is it repetitive movements? Floating? Is it ascent or descent?

If it's ascent, imagine that you are in a hot air balloon. See everything grow smaller and smaller as you climb high into the sky. The higher you go, the lighter you feel.

If it's descent, imagine being in an elevator. Watch the numbers decrease until you're at 0. Leave the elevator and imagine going into a room that causes you to feel completely relaxed.

You can make your own scenario. Just tell yourself that you are relaxing continuously.

Moving Meditations

Although many meditations require you to be still, you can meditate while you're moving. There are techniques that coordinate breathing with movements. You may also move randomly or dance around while listening to music. No matter what you do, you must move with the intent of focusing your mind.

Physical movement helps release pent up energy. It will help you feel freer when you are stuck in a rut. It will create harmony between your mind and body.

Some moving types of meditations are Qi Gong and Tai Chi. You can also meditate while doing something – even while washing the dishes. Fully concentrate on the task at hand.

Detachment

Meditation can make you more detached to allow you to see the problem (or situation) more objectively.

Close your eyes. Concentrate on the situation that's bothering you. Imagine that it is projected on a screen in front of your eyes. Watch the events, but play only what really happened instead of what you fear might occur. This will help reduce your fear so you can view it more realistically.

Replace yourself with another person. As an outsider, what would you advise the person on the screen? Remember what you tell him/her and act on your own advice.

You can increase your detachment about anything by changing how you portray it in your mind. By observing the situation through the perspective of an outsider, you allow yourself to respond differently.

Watching Thoughts

Release all external distractions. Close your eyes and turn your attention inwards. Observe all the thoughts that enter your awareness. Do not judge them. Do not block unpleasant thoughts or cling to pleasant ones.

Observe how one thought leads to another thought. This is your mind trying to distract you. Also, notice how your consciousness loses itself in what you think. Bring back your awareness as soon as you recognize this.

Detaching yourself from your thoughts enables you to have greater control over your responses. Do this whenever you feel overwhelmed by what you feel or think.

Koans

HSPs enjoy mental stimulation. Try Koans to keep yourself engaged.

A Koan is a paradoxical question that is not solved through reason or logic but by adopting a different perspective. You can find some Koans online but a meditation teacher may give you a unique Koan to ponder on.

For Koan meditation to be effective, you must stick to it even if you're having a difficult time comprehending it. Frustration is part of the experience and you will learn from it as well. Accepting the negative emotion will make it easier to manage, just like accepting trouble emotions make them lose their hold on you.

Don't be concerned that you can't solve it quickly. Even if you never find the answer, the Koan will create positive changes in you.

Reflect on the Koan as often as you could even if it's not your time to meditate. If you have a teacher, discuss your insights with him/her. If you don't have one, you can meditate on a resolution on your own.

Knowing the Knower

This is like the previous exercise because it causes mental stimulation. There is no right or wrong answer for this; the goals are to get to know yourself better and to learn how to direct your mind into positive directions.

Watch your thoughts without interacting with them. Ask yourself, "Who am I? Who is watching these thoughts? Who is meditating?" and other similar questions.

Do not demand an answer from your mind. Insights may arrive but you don't have to force them to. The questioning is the main exercise, not the answering.

If you do find yourself answering the questions, challenge your responses. If you replied, "The one who meditates is the mind in the body," follow up with another question such as, "How do I know that it is my own mind that is in this body?" and respond to that as well. Keep doing this until you arrived at a response that you are satisfied with.

You may create your own meditation routine as you become more familiar with how meditation works. If you want, write on a meditation journal so you can process what happened during your sessions. Discuss your experiences with a meditation teacher or fellow meditators so you can improve your techniques.

9 - Conclusion

High Sensitivity is a trait; whether it becomes a burden or a tool depends on how you handle it.

This book began with making you understand yourself more so that you can change your attitude about your trait and see it in a more positive light. As someone who recognizes the effects of inner thoughts, you will know that this is quite important in changing your destiny.

It gave numerous tips for addressing your needs and challenges in various aspects of your life. Although you may be able to learn these on your own, reading about them all in one place will make it easier for you to absorb.

As mentioned in the introduction, you must apply these tips for real learning to take place. We all learn best from experience.

Try teaching what you learned here to other HSPs and empaths to help them reach their own potentials. After all, the world needs help from people like you.

Continue learning and achieving. Enjoy more of life. You are the way you are for a good purpose, so find it and dedicate yourself to it. May this book be the trigger for many

9 - CONCLUSION

meaningful experiences and achievements.

Book 3 - Coping With Distress

Coping With Distress (Dealing with Negative Emotions, Empowerment, Handling Difficult People, Embracing Your Gift)

1 - Introduction

Hello there.

You've probably picked up this title because you feel that you're undergoing a lot of mood shifts. You've probably been called highly sensitive and are known to have abrupt changes in temperament.

Such is the daily struggle of an empath. You're one of a few blessed individuals that are capable of fully understanding the way someone else feels as if you were feeling it yourself. You're right in the driver's seat along with your family and friends.

Although this may sound like a blessing, it also comes with its sacrifices; usually in the form of stress. If you can share the happiness of other people, then you can most certainly share their woes as well. This makes stress for you a whole lot different from what it's like for anyone else.

This book is designed to help you cope with that part of your talent. Here, you'll find many tips and tricks to enable you to deal with the downsides so that you can fully enjoy the benefits of being a gifted empath.

From outlets to simple hacks, you'll learn the tools that have helped hundreds of other highly-sensitive people embrace their gift; advantages and disadvantages.

Thank you and peaceful reading!

2 - Defining an Empath

Take a good look at the people around you and close your eyes. Do you feel an empty room or a space full of auras and emotions? Can someone easily affect your mood just by feeling a certain way? Is it easy for you to feel compassion and empathy for those that are mistreated or are going through a rough time?

If you've answered yes to any of these questions, there's a large chance that you're highly sensitive to the feelings of others; sensitive enough to the point that you can feel the same way they do.

You've blurred the line between what you feel and what others feel, and just take in everything as your own. When someone radiates anger, you absorb it like a sponge and feel a burning sensation in your chest as well. When a hint of melancholy walks into the room, your spirit hides away and sobs quietly. For you, the feelings of other people end up becoming your feelings as well.

Besides this strange ability, you also exhibit characteristics that place you in certain situations that can cause a lot of stress. Being an empath is not easy, but your gift comes with a lot of other capacities.

The Characteristics of an Empath

Besides your natural ability to literally feel the same way other people do, you're also quite keen on the details. Small gestures, minuscule habits, and even those unnoticeable traits won't escape you. Your attention to details makes it easy for you to infer how one person is feeling, making you even more sensitive to their disposition.

Due to your sensitivity, there's also a large chance that you are moody. You be happy one minute and frustrated the next. Some people might even call you bipolar because of this. By no fault of yours, you instantly feel what other people feel. This is what causes you to change your disposition so quickly.

On top of that, your natural propensity to notice something wrong makes you an excellent listener. When you're faced with someone with a problem, your first task it to find the underlying cause of things because you feel for this person. In line with that, people find it easier to talk to you about what bothers them.

Naturally, you're also more drawn to quiet spaces. Because of the influence, other people can have on you, you find serenity in the absence of other people. Although that technically doesn't make you anti-social, you only long for the time when all you can feel are your own emotions.

This natural need to be alone allows you to grow inward, focusing on your personal talents. This makes empaths such as yourself to become creative in certain fields. Do you find yourself drawn to the arts? Are you fond of thinking freely and finding unusual solutions to usual problems? Your empathic tendencies cause you to become an innovative thinker.

In line with their sensitivity and preference for quiet places, you tend to avoid places that are buzzing with human activity. For you, these places can be draining and deafening. Imagine all those people and sensations that will come rushing towards you. This may be too overwhelming for you as a person.

If any of these descriptions are easy to relate with, then you have a special gift. Being able to see and feel the perspectives of others makes you an open-minded person capable of understanding both sides of any argument.

The Life Of An Empath

Imagine one of the biggest sporting events you've ever seen so far. The stands are full supporters, cheering on their favorite team. Imagine all that camaraderie and intensity rolled into one small setting.

When the team scores, there is an uproar of joy and excitement. The crowd gets on their feet and starts chanting in unison. Even if you're a bystander, you'll find yourself drawn into this crowd mentality. You tend to feel the excitement everyone else is feeling during that moment. There is no single fan. It's a large group of supporters that have one feeling.

For an empath such as yourself, life is one long sporting event where everyone else's emotions capture you and take you along for the ride, whether you want to or not.

You don't even have to activate this ability. It just happens. When someone exuding sadness comes into the room, you can just feel it and it takes over you as well. You could be in the middle of telling a funny story and suddenly lose all interest when a negative emotion disrupts your current mood.

It's a constant battle of being affected by the people around you, and it can be a tiring battle. Being pulled through different emotions against your will can be tiring and demanding.

But, it can be very rewarding, too. Your natural talent to see through the veil other people put up for themselves will win you an extraordinary amount of loyalty. People will trust your insights because they know you speak from the heart and you feel exactly the way they feel.

3 - Stress and the Empath

Take note that an empath isn't just capable of feeling the pain and happiness of other people. One thing they're very sensitive to is stress. On top of the stress they experience in their own lives, empaths also deal with the stress that other people radiate from themselves, creating a unique situation that requires attention.

What is stress?

Some people call it an emotion. Other people call it a state of mind. There are even those that call it a physical state of panic. What do you call stress?

On any other day, your body maintains a wide array of bodily processes that keep you alive. From releasing hormones to dictating heartbeat, your nervous system keeps track of all these actions, making sure everything is in order.

Now imagine an immediate physical threat to your well-being. Imagine an attack from a wild animal or a crook about to hurt you. In these situations, your nervous system shifts gears and makes some drastic changes in your body.

These changes will depend on your natural response to threats. Do you engage them or do you attempt to escape from them? Whatever the response may be, your body will reprogram your organs to accommodate this "fight or flight" response you have.

Depending on your nature, your body will downplay other processes to optimize others to increase your chances of survival. It will pump adrenaline through your bloodstream to improve physical performance. It will also halt other processes such as digestion and nutrient absorption to improve other processes and heighten your senses in response to the threat.

That's a reaction that has allowed our species to last this long. It's a good defense mechanism and all, but what if the threat involved isn't a physical threat?

What if the threat was a large business presentation to a potential client that could make or break your career? You can't fight or fly your way out of that, but your brain and nervous system will still consider this as a threat to your well-being.

When that happens, you're being prepared to physically engage a danger that cannot be engaged in such a manner. You can't fight your way through a big exam. You can't run from a much-needed job interview, but your body does it anyway. That is stress. It's your body responding to a perceived threat; regardless of the nature of the threat.

Your body is subjected to go into a defensive state to protect you from an intangible threat. Your mind cannot distinguish the difference between an animal attack and an attack to your finances or career. So, this mechanism becomes counterproductive and doesn't do you any good.

And since you can't use your elevated senses and heightened physical performance to engage these threats, they remain as threats. In as much as your brain perceives these as possible threats, it will maintain its defensive mode until you recognize the absence of the threat.

Now imagine being constantly on the defensive for a few days. Your body has optimized you for combat at the expense of normal function. You don't digest, breath, eat, sleep, and even think well.

It starts to take a toll on your body. You get less sleep. You lose focus. You feel more tired than usual and your presence of mind isn't just there at all. That is what stress does to you in the modern age.

In a way; you've got a medieval approach to dealing with modern problems. Sadly, this is not something you can turn off. It's how we humans were created.

Where does stress come from?

In this modern age of securities and borders, the likelihood of you needing to defend yourself against mortal danger have dropped significantly. Despite that, there are new sources of threats to your well-being.

One of the biggest contributors to your stress is your family. Your internal problems at home are the kind that stays with you even when you're not at home. Will you be able to pay this month's rent? There's a birthday party for your child in a few days, are you ready for the expenses? You have relatives that need financial help, are you able to help them?

It even doesn't have to be about money all the time. Are you able to spend enough time with your children to see them grow? Are you able to raise them with the right values? What about your parents and grandparents? Are you still able to spend time with them? How is your relationship with these people?

You can also incur stress from work. In fact, the delicate

scale of work-life balance could be one of the things that is afflicting you right now. How do you find the right amount of work to fulfill your career without sacrificing too much time with your loved ones? What is too much when it comes to your work responsibilities?

You'll be surprised to know that stress can also come from your friends. Yes, you love these people and you care for them. Thus, their mental state and emotions have a bigger bearing on how you feel as an empath.

Take note that these sources cause stress to you directly. Your problems and challenges at home, work and with friends can cause your body to go on the defensive.

Empath Stress

Your natural talent to be in other people's shoes doesn't just allow you to partake in their happiness and sorrow. You're also subject to their stress and anxieties.

Go back to imagining that great sports event with all those fans cheering. Imagine the favorite team throwing the game and making plenty of obvious mistakes. Imagine them letting the fans down.

Picture the frustration of so many people affecting each other, creating a massive ripple effect throughout the stands. Imagine the booing and the jeers coming from the disappointed fans. That is how an empath feels the stress of other people; all the time. That is probably what you feel daily.

It doesn't even matter if you've had a great rest last night. When someone experiencing a lot of stress comes within the vicinity, you can feel it in the air. Other empaths say it's like a prickling on the skin. Others say it's a general change in the temperature. It's an onset of negativity that can drain your energy and leave you in a slump by no choice of your own.

Second-Hand Stress

In a research effort done in Stockholm, it was found that the mental and emotional stress levels of the father directly affected the pregnancy of expected mothers, causing delays and complications during childbirth.

As an empath, you've probably experienced this tenfold in the presence of the people close to you. You can easily tell when other people are on the defensive and there's something eating at them. In turn, it starts to eat at you as well.

This is known as second-hand stress. You'll be surprised to know that you don't even have to be highly sensitive to become affected by second-hand stress. People can smell and even feel stress through verbal and non-verbal cues given off by someone who's undergoing their stress responses.

Imagine living with such a person for years. Imagine the amount of non-personal stress you'd be absorbing all the time. That's enough to change someone completely; and you most certainly don't want that much stress in your life, especially if it isn't even yours, to begin with.

In other cases, you don't even have to be living or dealing with someone in your immediate area to feel this kind of stress. If your social media feeds and other reading materials contain messages of stress and anxiety, your own anxieties aren't far behind.

You could have a friend on the other side of the world who would call you after a break-up and you'd feel just as bad as they would as you speak to each other. Your boss could be asking you where your colleague has been for the past few days and you can feel the anger and frustration coming from your supervisor.

Yes, you amplify the good times. Too bad you can't filter out the bad ones. But that doesn't mean you should live like that for the rest of your life. Your gifts also afford you natural defenses and techniques that can be done to counteract stress and second-hand stress in your life.

The Empath's Defenses

As an empath, carrying a stress ball and answering Sudoku puzzles isn't going to cut it. It may work for others but that may not be your cup of tea.

Your talent with emotions requires certain kinds of discipline and techniques to help you handle your stress and the stress of those around you.

Distance

The first and most obvious trick you should learn as an empath is putting distance in between you and your stressor.

Unlike other people that can't run away from their problems, you, as a gifted empath, can avoid second-hand stress by moving away from the people influencing your mood.

Experts say a good 15 to 20 meters from an area affecting you should be enough. Of course, that would also vary with how sensitive you are to the feelings and stress of other people.

One of the first things you should do when you feel the influence of others is to start moving away. After every few meters, take a close look at yourself to see if you're still affected.

However, you should be careful where you choose to run as well. You may end up running into an even larger cluster of emotions while getting away from one influence. It's always important to stop occasionally and gauge yourself.

One good thing about being an empath is that you don't have to talk to someone to get a gauge on how they feel. Most of the time, just seeing someone behave a certain way or just hearing they voice gives you an idea of how they're feeling.

Loving Yourself

In the case that you can't get away from someone's influence and you're stuck there, it's time for you to bust out some self-love.

One thing many empaths struggle with is the notion of accepting their gifts. You might have gone through this stage as well. You could also be working your way through it right this very moment.

You could be stressed out by the idea that you're a weak person, unable to handle the influence of other people. You could be thinking that this talent is only meant for those who are mature enough to handle its mantle.

One of the first things that you need to understand is the fact that your gift is not a reward for something you've done. It's a blessing that places you on a different level of understanding compared to other people.

You get to intimately share the emotions of other people despite not knowing them well. You get to feel what it's like to be a parent for the first time, almost all the time. You'll get to feel what it's like to be promoted when you've done nothing at all. You'll also fall in love with the world and the people in it on a regular basis.

All these wonderful experiences will also have their drawbacks. In your case, it's the drawback of feeling the pain, sorrow, and stress of others. It's knowing how stressed someone is over an argument with a loved one. It's also the pain of being far away from the people important to you.

You take the good and the bad together. When you've accepted both sides of the coin, dealing with your natural talents becomes almost as easy as breathing. Just think to yourself:

You were meant to feel more because you understand more.

When you've accepted this, your capacity to tolerate your stress and the stress of others grows tenfold.

4 - Creativity

Another thing that sprouts from your natural gift is a creative inclination. You don't just absorb emotions. You also absorb ideas and urges to let them out. It's a part of being you.

What can you do when you're feeling a rush of happiness at a wedding or being at someone's first birthday party? Besides talking about it to people close to you, you can turn to the arts as an outlet to express your emotions.

Write a song; and sing it. Write a poem, essay, or even a short story. Paint something. Dance. It doesn't matter what kind of outlet you use, if the one you choose allows you to express your creative soul and can give you fulfillment, then it's okay.

You'll be surprised to know what you can accomplish through the "mess" of emotions that go through you. Finding a creative outlet will turn this curse into a blessing that will realize your full potential.

Shielding

As simple as holding out an umbrella when it starts to rain, you can also protect yourself from picking up the emotions of other people with some shielding techniques.

Just as the name implies, these methods allow you to ignore incoming fluxes of other people and remain in your secure personal space. If you're new to your talent and lost in a sea of emotions and signals, these shielding techniques might take some getting used to, but in turn, will allow you to experience life like a normal person would.

Mental Imagery

This is one of the simplest forms of shielding you can afford; frankly, because it costs nothing. It just needs a different perspective.

Have you ever come across those picture puzzles entitled "Where's Waldo?"

These marvelously illustrated puzzles immerse you in large and detailed pictures showing busy streets, famous places, and tourist spots. These pictures are full of people minding their own business. It's easy to get lost in the immense effort put into the details.

With all those people and details, the puzzle urges you to just find one man, Waldo. He wears a red sweater and a red scarf, detailed with white stripes. The difficulty in finding Waldo in these pictures can be daunting and rewarding at the same time.

This is how you should look at mental imagery. In a sea of distractions, stress, emotions, voices, and attention, channeling all your attention onto one focal point will save you from the chaos.

The best part about this is that you don't even have to imagine Waldo. It could be any image you want. It could be your favorite painting or a memory of a calm and serene experience you've had before. The image should just be something that brings you peace.

When you start feeling the influence of other people, simply paint this image in your mind with your eyes closed. The more vivid the image you conjure, the better your focus becomes. Try this exercise for starters:

Find a quiet corner and make sure you're not facing anything busy. It doesn't matter if you're already suffering someone else's influence or if you're a clean slate.

When you're in that corner, don't immediately jump into your meditation. You need to be in the right mindset. This will take a while to accomplish. Understand that whether you're an empath or not, your mind has different states.

When you're afflicted with the emotions and stress of other people, it will take some time move from a confused and defensive state to a state of calm.

To do that, close your eyes and try to remember that mental image of yours, but don't just paste the picture into your mind. Construct that image from the bottom up.

Was it morning or evening in that mental image of yours? Where was this image located? Was it at home or was it out? Were you with anyone during this memory or image? What was the weather like? Was there a hint of sunshine or was it raining? Start with the general details and create an environment for this mental image of yours.

Once you've created the general details, now you can start with the more important parts of this image. Who were you with? Were you alone? What were you doing in this image? Was there food involved? What was the general activity during that time?

The more specific you get, the clearer the image becomes. What were you wearing? What were the colors involved? What accessories were you wearing? As you bring these details together, the full picture comes to mind. When that happens, now is the time to really bring it home.

What were you feeling during that time? Were you happy? What was the general emotion of the moment? With your natural talent, the feelings should flow into you naturally. And in all the nostalgia you're enjoying, you've probably forgotten something.

You're no longer afflicted with the emotions of those around you! You've become wrapped around this image long enough that you've sunk away from the environment and have developed a small bubble for your own thoughts to grow!

That is the power of meditation. When done properly, everything else just fades away. With repeated practice, the shifting states of your mind become easier to control. It even develops to the point that you can meditate on your image almost anywhere!

5 - Boundary Setting

Besides turning your thoughts inward, you can also use your talents to set a boundary on the influence of others. This comes in handy when you're with someone that's emotionally-charged. As an empath, there's a high chance their feelings will rub off on you.

This is done by visualizing a circle around you. Think of this circle as going around your whole body, protecting you from emotions and ideas that aren't your own. This circle of light will serve as an imaginary boundary that will just as good as a physical one.

Despite this being a mental activity, your mind is powerful enough to commit to this boundary you're setting. Despite that, the boundary won't work unless you add more detail to it.

Picture this circle of light around you as a set of rules that you apply to yourself. Within that circle, determine all the thoughts and emotions that belong to you. Consider your own worries and anxieties and mark them as your own. These things within the circle are all coming from you without the influence of others.

On that same note, everything outside the circle doesn't belong to you, and thus, should be discarded. These are the things that you pick up from other people.

- Noticing someone hit the table in anger

- Hearing a hint of aggression from someone over the phone

- Getting a glimpse of a frown

- Sensing some authority from a speaker

All these things do not go through that circle, and if it's not within the circle, they shouldn't go through.

By delineating what is within you and what comes towards you, you can immediately filter the emotions and vibes that come your way. By doing so, you can block off any negativity coming your way because you aren't focused on dealing with the emotions of others but on dealing with whatever is in your circle.

When these boundaries become clear and more established, this circle of light isn't just a circle anymore. It becomes a wall that protects you from influences that you do not welcome into your person.

Mindfulness Meditation

Considered a useful tool even for non-empaths, mindfulness harnesses your mind's capacity to shift focus. For an empath, this could be difficult with all the influences you can absorb. But with proper training, you can develop this skill and use it as instant relief from the many emotions you encounter every day.

Like mental imagery, mindfulness meditation forces you to stop thinking about feelings that aren't yours as you shift focus to the sensations that you're personally feeling right that moment.

It begins the same way, by finding a nice quiet corner wherein you can focus. This time, instead of bringing an image to mind, you appreciate your surroundings and live in the moment.

You begin by closing your eyes and focusing on one area at a time. Start with your feet. As you're seated with your eyes closed, focus your attention to your feet. Don't just feel the floor through your shoes. Feel your toes inside your socks. You can choose to wiggle your toes if it helps you focus on them.

As you focus on your feet, recognize the sensations you're feeling. Are your socks warm enough around your feet? How does the fabric feel on your foot? Be sure to account for both feet as you feel them on the ground.

Once you're done with the feet, move upward to your legs. How does the fabric of your pants or shorts feel against your legs? Is it letting your skin breath or is it constricting? Are your bare legs exposed? Is there a breeze coming through your legs? Don't comment on the status of your legs, but focus on what your legs are feeling right that moment.

Do the same thing with your hands and arms as you move upward. If your hands and arms are resting on something, try to put those sensations into words as you meditate. As you move through various parts of your body, you'll notice that you're slowly living in the moment while realizing the many sensations that you usually take for granted.

That is the premise of mindfulness. You forget about what you're thinking and just focus on what is going right that moment. This may be hard to do if you're a beginner but it gets easier with repetition and constant practice.

One thing that could disrupt your meditation is your own

mind. It is inevitable to sometimes drift into your own thoughts in the middle of meditation and start to think inward. But you shouldn't let this disrupt your rhythm. Slowly remind yourself of what you're doing and start over. There's nothing wrong with getting lost in your thoughts, you just need to know how to guide yourself back and refocus.

Interestingly, you don't always have to focus on the moment and the sensations you're feeling. Mindfulness meditation can also be done with your breath.

Instead of thinking about your various body parts, you can visualize your lungs and your diaphragm as you take in breaths. Visualize the air coming into your lungs as it is absorbed into your bloodstream. Take as many breaths as you want to create the full image in your head.

The whole process should not take more than five minutes to fully refresh your senses. At the end of the meditation, you're back in the moment without any thought about other people's emotions and stress.

6 - Protective Clothing

You'll be surprised to know that the influence of other emotions on you isn't just invisible lights going back and forth in the air. You're really picking up scents, actions, gestures, and even electrical signals given off by other people.

There are certain types of clothing materials and items that can help deflect negative onsets coming your way. Most empaths and experts have come up with two important items to help get that done:

Silk

Silk isn't just a nice fabric to sleep on. It's also recognized for its ability to keep things inward. That's what makes it a good bed sheet, but an even better shield. It will keep your own emotions and vibrations inside while keeping out other influences from your mood.

You don't have to cover your whole body in silk. Though, simply carrying silk around is good enough. You can carry around a scarf or a hat that as some silk on it.

Mirrors

What better way to bounce things off than the one thing

that could bounce off the light? Although wearing a large mirror in public isn't a good idea, you can wear a smaller one as a pendant or necklace. If you're male and don't like the idea of accessorizing with a mirror, you could just keep one in your bag.

Empath Magic

What's the use of a talent it you're always sick because of it? One thing that you should enjoy as an empath is the capacity to understand others on a level of understanding that almost matches a personal knowledge.

On top of understanding others so well, your talent also affords you a deeper appreciation of de-stressing techniques. When an influx of comfort comes your way, you tend to feel it more than others do.

Here, you will uncover a few habits and experiences that will help you unclog your emotional drains and help you cope with your stress, which usually stems from the stress of other people.

Zooming In

Usually, when we understand a lot about someone, we look

at them from a different perspective; a larger one at that. When we care about someone, we don't just look at present experiences. We look at futures with this person. This sometimes will affect you with stress because of all the challenges that lay ahead of you and the ones you love.

This is what makes zooming in a very good technique for the empath under stress. Instead of worrying about the things that will affect you and the people around you, start focusing on what you have now.

Consider the small things for a change. Instead of worrying about college funds for your child during their small birthday party, look at the smile on their faces. Be thankful that you're there to see them have the time of their lives.

Don't brood over the immense challenges that you and others face at a certain moment. Be thankful for the moments you have the chance to sit down with someone and talk like good friends.

If anyone can benefit from looking at the good side of things, then an empath like yourself should, even more, reap from how this change in perspective can also alter your state of mind.

You may be surrounded by stress and anxiety that isn't your own, but you have plenty to be thankful for as an empath. Your talents allow you to see the world through other people's eyes. You get to know people far beyond the reach of their closest friends and relatives. That's plenty to be thankful for.

Junking the Routine

As a highly-sensitive person, you're more inclined to plan things ahead of time to avoid stress and stressing out the people around you. This may be counter-productive if you really want to avoid negativity and frustration. What happens when something goes wrong and the plan doesn't really work out?

It's always better to go with the flow. When you're not expecting anything, almost anything can surprise you and bring in plenty of positivity in your life.

Go on that sudden trip when your friends ask you to come with them. Surprise your family with a short trip to the beach. Go home and make a fancy dinner for the family for no apparent reason. Not only will these things make you happy, but it will also make the people around you happy, which in turn, you'll get to feel as well.

Simmer Down at Night

When the day is done, you're full of so many things which are either good or bad. Before going to bed, take some time to close your eyes and let all that go. As you're about to lie down, close your eyes and look back at the day you've had and highlight the important things that happened to you.

Be thankful for the good that came in and let go of the things that didn't go your way. One thing you're good at is to take things to heart, all the way to bed. Letting all those things go before you sleep will help you sleep better and give you a fresh clean slate when you wake up the next day.

Check Yourself Constantly

While you're so busy absorbing everything around you, you can sometimes forget to ground yourself and regain your bearings. You can easily get lost in the emotions and influence of others that you may end up forgetting yourself.

When you're active, take a few minutes to consider yourself. Find some quiet time and ask yourself a few questions:

How am I right now? Am I all right? How am I feeling? Is this feeling from me or from someone else?

When you're able to answer these questions, you place yourself in an objective perspective, allowing you to better process the things you're feeling. In such a state, you can focus on what you need to do instead of dealing with what is going on around you.

Bedtime Fun

As an empath, your talents also allow you to live life to the fullest. This is because you're capable of seeing the deeper meaning in things; especially if you're with someone.

This is how sex can take on a new level. Going beyond the confines of physical pleasure, you treat coitus as an emotional adventure just as much as it is a treat for the flesh. You develop deep bonds of trust and affection for your partner and get to release your inhibitions as you take care of your carnal desires.

Thus, sex should be one of your best stress busters; not just because of obvious reasons.

An empath such as you doesn't engage in coitus for the

physical release. Through sex, you also clean your slate and recharge your affection with someone. By being intimate, you get to affirm your emotional prowess and satisfy your urges, while getting a rush of pleasure.

If sex is known as a great method for regular people to de-stress, it should be an optimum tool for an emotionally-charged empath such as yourself.

Pool Time

This may surprise you, but research has shown that dipping yourself in a suitable body of water has great effects to the mind under stress.

You may already know that any form of rigorous physical activity can reduce stress. This is because the body produces endorphins during the process, and these are your happy hormones. They are known to counteract the effects of stress and bring the body back to a state of homeostasis.

On that same note, swimming does all that and probably a little more. This is because the nature of the exercise is a natural cycle of tension, relaxation, and breathing.

This combination of the processes during swimming act as

ideal outlets for your fight-or-flight reactions. It coaxes your body into thinking you're getting away from danger. Once you've had your fill of swimming, you're full of endorphins and oxygen. You've also given almost every part of your body a full workout.

Another point you can consider is the fact that swimming is a repetitive exercise with predictable outcomes. When you're stressed over the emotions and problems of other people, diving into the pool will also exercise your sense of control over your situation, balancing out your thoughts.

Terrific Tea

Although a healthy diet is obvious given for a better stress response and physical state, certain food and drinks can help ease your tension when you're already suffering from someone else's affliction; you can start with tea for that.

To be more specific, drink black tea. This variant is rich in antioxidants that aren't just good to fight the signs of aging. It also lowers the risk of heart attack and various forms of cancer.

In relation to stress, black tea helps soothe the mind and re-lax the senses. When prepared properly, black tea can immediately calm your nerves the moment an onset of afflictions starts getting to you.

Humor

This will probably be the best tool that you can use to combat stress. In the right conditions, you (empaths in general) could be the happiest people on the planet.

Imagine yourself at a good comedy bar. They have a regular who's good with the tough crowds. He busts out a few starters and you're already giggling in your seat. You can also feel the hints of laughter and smiles coming from the other people in the room.

Once he's warmed up, he hits you with his best punch-lines and now has the whole room bursting with laughter. Being an empath in that kind of situation is one of the best experiences your gift can offer. You don't just feel your appreciation of humor, you also take in the happiness and amusement of everyone else you're with.

That's the beauty of humor. Laughter has been known to immediately remedy the physical manifestations of stress. You could probably attest to that as well. A good joke or two might have erased any notion of fatigue you might have had.

Humor also serves as a great distraction if your mind is already full of everyone else's worries. If something funny enough can cause you to laugh, that's proof enough that it's restoring your nerves and your composure.

It's good to indulge in a good laugh or two. Go visit the local open mic night at the bar or watch some stand-up videos on the internet. It doesn't matter if you're a fan of slapstick or dark humor. If it amuses you, it will relieve your stress and leave you more satisfied with yourself.

The Hand Rub

When you're caught off-guard and inside a maelstrom of stress and emotion and it's impossible to walk away, you may find yourself cornered and helpless. These situations could completely drain you and leave you emotionally devoid and unwilling to communicate to others.

For those cases, an immediate dose of comfort will work wonders. Immediately put the palms of your hands together and begin rubbing them. The goal here is to rub them long enough to make them warm. Don't use lotions or creams or anything, just rub the bare skin.

When your hands become warm, place them over the lids of your eyes while they're closed. This simulates the feeling you get on a cold night with a warm blanket all over your head. The darkness and the warmth will provide you with a small amount of comfort, hopefully, long enough for you to regain your bearings.

Pet Magic

You'll be surprised to know that a study of about 100 women in the United States discovered that women who owned dogs all had lower blood pressures than women who didn't.

High blood pressures could result from stress. A spike in pressure is the body's way of getting more oxygen and nutrients to the other parts to help them perform better during an emergency. So, it's safe to say that owning a dog helps you deal with stress.

Look beyond the expenses and the time necessary for taking care of such an animal. In this world full of stressors and threats, a good stress reliever is never too expensive or needy.

But it's not the owning that helps relieve stress. It's the experience of having one. Wouldn't you like to come home to a pet that's always happy to see you? This is true even if they left you a surprise on the carpet?

Wouldn't you like to have someone just come up to you and ask for a hug or a treat or a pet or even a belly rub? Feeling needed and important are some of the biggest needs in a person's life. Getting a pet works towards fulfilling those needs.

It's understandable if you're allergic or if your apartment doesn't allow pets. You don't really need to own one. Visit a friend who owns a pet and spends a few minutes playing with them and petting them. It serves as a great distraction and an even better pick-me-up after a long day.

Regaining Control

Another reason empaths feel more stress than normal is because they get so lost in the experiences that their gifts afford them. One time they could be incredibly happy and then go completely blank when someone else just walks into the room.

This is especially true for new empaths that have just recognized their gifts and are still struggling to control them. It's more of a control issue, and the issue is you have very little control over the situation.

Hence, shifting your focus to something you can control is an ideal way to deal with empath's stress. When you feel overwhelmed and out of the pilot' seat, pause for a while and look for something that depends on your influence.

Make plans for the rest of the way. Where will you go after work? What will you have for dinner? What will you buy yourself later? How many beers are you going to finish? Who will you hang out with later? Organize something simple that you can execute with minimal effort.

Even a simple omelet dinner made by hand is a good idea if you planned and executed it yourself. These kinds of achievements will return that sense of control you think you lost when you started noticing and imbibing someone else's stress.

7 - Alternative Remedies for Empaths

Acupuncture

You might be wondering as to why something as old as acupuncture could be used to soothe an empath such as yourself. With years of research backing it, acupuncture has found a new relevance in the modern world.

Research has shown that acupuncture has positive effects on stress in regular people. Knowledge about pressure points allows specialists to zero in on target areas and release tension in people.

What is Acupuncture?

You may already have an idea of what acupuncture is through modern media. Can pins and needles go into someone to help them recover? It may sound strange but there is deep knowledge behind this practice.

Having originated from China, acupuncture is the practice of using pins to hit certain points on the body. It is one of the vital components of classic Chinese medicine, circling around the concept of chi and pressure points.

This theory proposes that certain nerve endings on the skin are connected to various organs in the body, helping to regulate bodily processes. When something is wrong around a certain area, the process involves stimulating a certain point on the skin that is connected to the part will relieve the symptoms and allow the body to heal faster.

From this standpoint, acupuncture branches out into other sub-theories and practices, all focusing on the presence of these pressure points.

When done by a specialist with the proper equipment, acupuncture has been known to alleviate pain and ease out stress from patients. Despite not being formally recognized as an exact science, many people are looking for this method as a form of alternative medicine.

Acupuncture for Empaths

For you and your natural gifts, acupuncture can be taken a step further. Because you can naturally amplify external stimuli that come your way, acupuncture may become one of the best de-stressing tools for you.

It is important that you find a licensed specialist within your area should you want to try acupuncture. Because of its popularity, many practitioners are willing to forego proper training and just set up a clinic to get a share of the market.

You want a properly trained professional that doesn't just execute well. They should also be able to explain their processes and the supposed effects of their treatment methods.

Music Therapy

You don't even have to be in the same room with someone to know how they feel. Sometimes, just listening to the music they make can affect the way you feel as well. Thus, you also have a special bond with music. It's not just an auditory experience for you. It's like the performer is right there with you, sharing their emotions in one of the most honest ways possible.

This is the magic of music because there are messages in music. Placing the obvious lyrics and melodies aside, you can zero in on that message and fully appreciate a song that comes your way.

This is also why the wrong choice in music can throw you off balance. It doesn't even matter what your taste in music is. You can get as much of a sad vibe from a love ballad as well as from a heavy metal track.

Given this tendency, you can use music to soothe your nerves and cleanse your aura. All it takes is the right set of notes to get the job done.

Use your natural sensitivity and preferences to your advantage. Don't just listen to something because it sounds good. Gauge how you feel when you listen to a certain track. Is it upsetting you or is it uplifting? Open a blank playlist and add those tracks that literally change the way you feel.

Weightless – Marconi Union

Not sure where to start looking for music? You can start with this track. What makes this piece so useful for de-stressing is the fact that the effects of this song have been backed by scientific research.

Sound therapists and scientists have found that this track can reduce anxiety levels in people by more than 50% in most cases. It's the most effective track tested and has produced better results than any other soothing track. That includes tracks of ambient environments and meditative tracks.

Of course, music is a personal experience which doesn't mean that ambient tracks and meditative chants aren't effective at all. As an empath, you only need to sample these things for yourself and see what works and what doesn't.

Aromatherapy

Besides being sensitive to music, your other senses can notice and pick up other stimuli quite easily; your nose being no exception to this capacity. You've also probably noticed that you're not comfortable around certain smells, regardless if they're pleasant or not. You've probably found the perfume of some of your friends a bit distracting and nauseating.

This is because you intercept the feelings of other people through your senses. Your natural gift allows you to pick up more than just scents. That's why you are probably very meticulous with the scents that you put on yourself as well. Do you mostly go for neutral scents? Or is there a certain smell that makes you feel at home?

With the right fragrances, you can customize your environment (or your immediate surroundings) to influence your sense of smell in a positive manner. But don't just rely on perfumes and bath soaps. Aromatherapists use essential oils made from various herbs and flowers to induce certain states. Try these scents for their stress-reducing capacities:

- Chamomile

- Bergamot

- Lavender

- Rose

- Ylang-Ylang

These are popular fragrances that are said to reduce anxiety in people. You don't necessarily have to cover yourself in these oils. You can apply them by several methods.

First, you can add a few drops of these oils to your clothing. They can be dabbed on your sleeves and collar so that you can take in their fragrances when you move about. You can also empty a few drops into your bath to add some fragrance to your washing. These oils stick to the body and absorb easily.

Finally, you can also get a diffuser that can spread the fragrance of the oils around the whole room, enveloping you in its essence. You won't have to frequently apply to enjoy the aroma. It will be all around you as you move about.

They key is to make these scents available at the onset of discomfort. Because they're easy to bring, essential oils are ideal for the workplace and on the road where you can't choose the people who enter your field of influence.

Hypnosis

Don't mistake this for staring at a swinging pendulum while someone is talking softly to you. Hypnosis has proven to be quite an effective and direct approach to dealing with stress.

It's twice as effective when it is used on someone with talents such as yours. This is because hypnosis bypasses your clouded thoughts and emotions and immediately puts you in a relaxed state that can succumb to the power of suggestion.

Today, this method has become widely accepted and used by many professionals that a lot on their plates. It helps them clear their minds and focus on what is important.

Fortunately, you can go about hypnosis in one of two ways:

Professional Hypnosis

The traditional method of hypnosis is done under the guidance of a specialist. Be sure to do your due diligence before approaching a clinic or a hypnotist. Check their records and their permits lest you get conned.

Legitimate hypnosis will take place in a quiet room where it's just you and the specialist. Through various methods such neuro-linguistic programming and effective body language, the specialist will put you in a state of deep relaxation.

You'll be surprised to know that hypnotism is a profession that requires a license. Specialist spend years of study and practice to help other people cope with their personal struggles. This is considered a powerful hypnosis technique.

Self-Hypnosis

Being the more recent emergence of the two, self-hypnosis rests on the assumption that you can place yourself in a state that accepts suggestion even without the presence of a licensed specialist.

You will probably want to try this method first to see if hypnotism is suitable for you and your gifts. It starts by placing yourself in a place with minimal distractions.

Once in a quiet area, find a space or an object on the ceiling on which to focus. This could be a panel or a light bulb. It could also be a lizard if you're comfortable with that.

Next, look straight forward with a level head and begin rolling your pupils upward, trying to look at the object at the ceiling. Try not to move your head upward and let your eyeballs do the rolling.

Roll your eyeballs up to the point that you feel a slight strain within your sockets. That means you've brought them to the farthest point. As you roll your eyes upward, take in a deep breath. Make it one very deep breath all the way to the point that strains your eyes.

When you've reached that point, hold your breath for a few moments and then exhale. As you exhale, return your eyes to their normal position as well. Rest your eyes for a few more seconds then repeat the process one more time.

At the end of this second eye rolling, begin to close your eyes as you exhale to prepare for relaxation. As your eyes are closed, imagine your feet slowly rising in the air along with the rest of your body. You've become weightless as you slowly move upward.

As you imagine yourself floating upward, you're taking yourself to the top of a hill. Once you're at the top, visualize the hill looking down at a valley. That's where you're taking yourself.

Imagine ten steps down to this valley from the top of the hill. Start taking yourself down those steps. Count the steps as you take them. You're still feeling weightless at this point as you move downward.

When you reach the last step, you're supposed to have reached the state of relaxation necessary for a suggestion. This is where you take a personal statement and claim it to be true to yourself.

Consider what you're feeling in the now, and focus on what you want to happen after this session of self-hypnosis. Form the statement in your mind as you reach that last step at the bottom of the hill.

If you're clouded by the feelings and stress of those around you, then claim that "when I open my eyes, my slate will be cleaned".

If you're suffering from personal stress, then you can claim that "I will have a clear head when I open my eyes".

It all depends on what you want to accomplish at the end of the hypnosis. Remember that you need to be specific about what you want. Hypnosis doesn't operate on vague suggestions like "everything will be all right". Zero in on how you want to feel and your mind will make it happen.

When you've reached the bottom of the hill and finished the ten steps to get there, begin repeating that formed message to yourself. You can choose to say it loud like a mantra or say it in your mind as a form of meditation. Picture yourself smiling and feeling better at the bottom of the hill as you recite your message.

Remain in this state for about ten minutes, and simply repeating that mantra at the bottom of that imaginary hill. Feel your muscles relax and your tension disappear as you've already shifted focus from your stress to your image on the hill.

When you're ready to open your eyes, take one more breath and slowly open as you exhale. You'll be surprised to find that you've cleared your mind and you're now twice as ready to deal with other people.

Color Therapy

If you're not a fan of hypnosis or you think it doesn't work for you, maybe a simpler approach could be more effective; like one that uses colors.

This technique was developed with the notion that colors affect us on more than just an aesthetic level. The vibrations given off by colors can cause us to feel certain ways because of how the light bounces off them.

It's in this practice that sales-oriented people usually wear purple or pink to sales meetings with clients in hope that the color makes their targets easier to convince. When we see colors, our brain makes certain connections that make certain decisions and feelings easier to come by.

For stress on your emphatic level, it would help if you incorporated certain colors in your environment, namely:

- Green – meant for appeasing tension build-ups in the nerves.

- Yellow – meant for clearing the mind and realigning

focus.

- Blue – meant for easing the troubled mind amidst confusing emotions.

- Indigo – meant for counteracting anger and replacing it with more docile emotions.

From this point, it's a simple matter of finding ways to incorporate these colors into your immediate area. The first and most obvious way would be to wear clothing items that sport these colors. Given that, you need to make sure that you can see these colors on you. It won't work if they're the color of your undergarments.

Other than that, they can also be placed in your curtains or furniture. Buying pieces with these colors makes them easy to find within your home, making your personal space a more effective escape from stress.

Another creative method is to choose these colors when it comes to food. If possible finding fruits and food items in these colors help make them more accessible to you.

When they're all around you, their influence grows as well. Despite that, it's important that you see these colors and not just sit comfortably with the knowledge that the colors are there. For the therapy to work, you need to be surrounded by and experiencing these colors.

8 - Dealing with Emotional Vampires

It's one thing to have to experience the emotions and stress of other people. It's a completely different thing to deal someone that literally drains you of your energy to do that.

What is an emotional vampire?

Have you ever been to a wedding and found someone who just didn't move along with the general splendor and happiness of the moment? Have you ever seen someone that just makes everyone lose interest in what was happening? Have you ever dealt with someone that can manage to find everything wrong with something good and make you feel terrible just with the things they say?

Those statements describe the capacities of an emotional vampire. They're called such because they can suck the emotional life out of someone in exchange for reinforcing their own principles and ego. They do these things to make themselves feel better.

You can find them all around you; even at home. They come in all shapes and sizes. They could be in the office with you or even waiting for you at home with the rest of your family.

They may know they're draining you or be completely oblivious to it, but their effects are just the same. These people could greatly contribute to your stress as an empath because, on top of dealing with their emotions, you're also dealing with their adverse effect on your own state of well-being.

The Five Vampires

There's not just one kind of emotional vampire. The ability to drain your emotional power comes in different shapes in sizes, just like there are different kinds of empaths that share your gift.

The Permanent Victim

These are the kinds of people that are eternally on the losing end of everything. Whether it is work or home, they're not happy and they think it's because they're unlucky.

Although it's true that life is full of challenges that will put you down, a victim will always think that they're destined to fail, get hurt, get left behind, get cheated and anything else you can think of.

With that in mind, they always need someone to coddle

them. They are in this constant state of neediness that needs to be filled by someone more successful and stable that them. They are incapable of motivating themselves. Being around these kinds of people can be very draining, especially if they come back to you for the same reasons all the time.

No amount of motivation or advice will convince them that their life will change. They are stuck in the notion that they will always lose out and will need someone to take care of them.

They can be draining for you because you can feel their despair. It's not an act. But they're so wrapped up in their misery that they're no longer capable of picking themselves up to look for better days.

As an empath, you'd want to help them the best you can, but nothing you do will ever change their minds. This brings about a sense of defeat and helplessness that could end up consuming you, potentially bringing you over to their side.

To deal with this kind of vampire, learn to acknowledge their despair and draw the line on your contribution. Confirm with them that you understand what they're going through but also be firm that you won't involve yourself that much.

This can be challenging especially if this is a friend or family member, as you would want to help as much as you can. Despite that, you need to set your limits lest you become another vampire yourself.

The Self-Absorbed Narcissist

If there are vampires that feel who life is the worst, there are also those that think life owes them everything. These people love themselves so much that they crave attention and praise.

This could be the star at the office that looks down on everyone. It could also be that relative that seems to have everything figured out. These are people that always put themselves before others.

They're entitled to the best that life has to offer at the expense of another person's happiness. You'll notice them by their loudness and drive to be ahead of the rest. This causes them to lack empathy and compassion for those that are struggling.

You'll immediately be drawn to them because they radiate too much confidence. You'll see that they can handle themselves rather well until the point that you disagree with them. Any challenge to their superiority will result in aggression or even complete shut-outs from them. They can never be wrong in their eyes.

Dealing with a narcissist will drain your energy because you'll never win against one. They will be confident enough to say that you need to be doing this and that for them, but when you try to put things in perspective, they'll call you an antagonist.

When you've labeled a narcissist in your life, try to not to get drawn in by their confidence. They're naturally capable of inspiring people to like them because they can handle themselves quite well in public.

When they begin talking about themselves, remember your own expectations for yourself and draw the line when they start to challenge what you hold important to yourself.

The Thug Boss

These are the people that seem to know how to do everything right. They want something to go in a certain way and will not rest until it is done the way they want it to be done.

To get their way, they'll insert their own opinions almost all the time, usually in arguments meant to belittle the perspectives of other people. You'll notice that these people will be able to say something unpleasant about almost everything that isn't originally their idea.

You'll find them if they give the impression that they know what's best for you as if they've lived in your shoes long enough. You, of all people, know what it's like to feel the same way other people feel. This is where they start draining you.

As an empath, you want to give them the attention and recognition so as not to hurt their feelings, but these controlling people will use guilt, logic, information, and even emotional blackmail to get what they want.

As a result, you will feel used and owned. You'll tend to match things up to their perspective most of the time and feel put down when you're about to have an original idea.

On that same note, these people hate to be corrected as well. They will try their hardest to prove that you're wrong and will use every trick in the book to make you feel that it was a bad idea trying to go against their own iron-clad knowledge.

The trick to dealing with these kinds of people is to assert your own side and recognize whatever validity they claim to have on their side. Never try to control them because they will be more than happy to engage you and never yield.

Simply recognize what they can offer and move on with what you think is right. As an empath, you have more emotions and ideas than most people can offer. Live with that fact and don't let anyone tell you otherwise.

The Melodramatic

Whether it's a skinned knee or a bad salad, these people will blow things out of proportion. It comes from their need to validate what they feel. In their eyes, everything is important. Everything that happens needs everyone's attention and care.

They usually blow things up when it suits them best. They will use a simple cold that "almost killed them" to explain why they're late for work. They will use a break-up to justify sub-par quality at work. They will make excuses to make it seem that it's all right for them to behave a certain way because they're "dealing with something."

Their constant drama drains you. When all this person talks about is how important their problems are, you'll feel defeated and helpless amidst all their complaining. You're afraid to invalidate and challenge their claims because you know you're running the risk of them blowing up your opinion into something more sinister than you intended.

To deal with this kind of person, draw strength from your own experiences. If you know something is out of proportion, keep your calm and don't get drawn in by the drama. These people run on hyperventilation and enhanced emotions. Adding your own emotions into the mix will only have catastrophic consequences.

If they need to commit to something, be sure to state the rule and the fact that there are no excuses to be made. If they need to come into work, then make it clear. If you need them to do something, let them know that you're counting on them and what's at stake. Acknowledge the presence of drama in their lives but remind them that the world doesn't revolve around their issues alone.

The Expert

Have you ever been around someone who had to be right all the time? Whether it's work-related or not, there are those people that just need to let out their thoughts and make sure that everyone in the room agrees with them? That's how the expert works.

They don't live off the recognition. They live off the thrill of debate. These people do not want to prove that they're right. They want to prove that everyone else is wrong.

To do just that, they'll voice out offense at the things you say. You'll be a permanent tyrant in their eyes or an ignorant bystander that doesn't know any better. As they claim their righteousness, they'll call you out.

This could be that supervisor at work who can't take criticism well. It could be that friend who never seems to get tired challenging your views. It could also be someone close who just gets too much criticism at the office that they feel the need to be acknowledged at home when they can be themselves.

It will be difficult for you as an empath to deal with these kinds of people. You may have the best intentions but they'll overlook that and find something wrong with what you tell them. You could come off as nice and understanding but if you think they're wrong, they will brush you off and call you insensitive and crass.

The Sad Truth

Can you make it so that you avoid vampires for the rest of your life? Sadly, these people will be anywhere you go. They're a natural part of life. Think of them as people going through their own developmental stages.

On top of their usual problems, telling them that you're an empath will only make things worse. They'll never understand that you're trying to reach out. They'll probably think you're trying to stand out on your own and get some satisfaction out of their situation.

Be patient but hold your ground. When someone is testing your patience and draining your energy, distract yourself and shift your focus to something else. Your energy as an empath is a very precious resource. Spend it on the people that matter.

9 - Conclusion

At this point, you're now ready to go back into the world and ready to meet new emotions and people. With the techniques and tricks that you've learned, you're better at handling yourself with others and thus, become more helpful to those that need to feel understood.

You're now able to enjoy the best that your talents can offer. By controlling your reactions and checking yourself constantly, you can minimize the damage done by second-hand stress and other people's frustrations. By applying alternative methods, you're capable of dealing with your daily issues a lot better, making you more self-sufficient as an empath.

In turn, a self-sufficient empath becomes an inspiration to other empaths. Share your knowledge with other people you know that possess the same gift as you. Help someone else accept their gifts and learn how to deal with the downsides as you have.

And finally, be a blessing to those that need you. There's a reason you have that gift. It's meant for you to open the eyes of other people and let them see through the different perspectives that you hold as an empath.

Book 4 - Empath Healing Made Easy For Beginners

Empath Healing Made Easy For Beginners (Handling Sociopaths and Narcisissists, Protect Yourself From Manipulation, Self-Aware Energy)

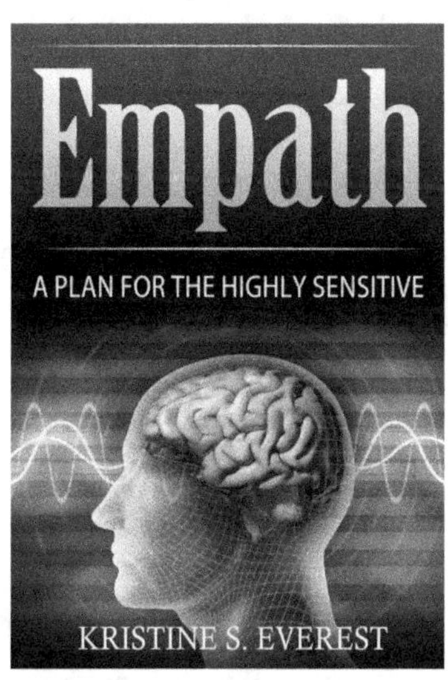

1 - Introduction

What Is Empathy?

Defined simply, empathy and healing may not readily form an association. However, there are many things that connect one to the other. To better understand this, let's begin by taking a closer look at each.

Empathy

This is a person's ability to understand and even share in another person's emotions, as well as feelings. Think of it as being able to put yourself into someone else's shoes and be able to experience their emotions as well.

Healer

This is a person who heals. These are people who are skilled in a particular type of therapy and are capable of treating different illnesses through various means. Some healers call upon divine help when working, whilst there are those who try to manipulate the body by engaging the mind and spirit.

Empathy and Healing: The Connection

Empathic people and healers share the ability to resonate

with others and tune into their energies. For most empaths, this can happen involuntarily. There are those who have more control over this ability, however.

What an empathic person can do, especially if they take it upon themselves to further their knowledge and improve this inherent skill, is to scan another person's psyche for their feelings or for past, present, and future life occurrences. Their heightened sensitivity makes them more adept at catching the smallest of changes in people especially in the energy they are emitting. In healing, energy is important.

Empaths can experience this towards their immediate family, their children, close friends, work associates and other acquaintances, their pets, the plants that they keep, and even with complete strangers. Some may even experience this towards inanimate objects in that they're able to sense its history. Empathy is not bound by time or space.

This is why some empaths can actually feel the energy of people from a distance. There are also empaths who are more in-tune with animals and are capable of communicating with them on a more profound level; think of The Horse Whisperer or someone like Cesar Milan, who can read the energies of the dogs he works with.

Healers and empaths also share a deep sense of knowing. They are more compassionate, understanding and considerate of others. A heightened sense of self-awareness is also common. Though there are also those who manifest these abilities even at a young age, but do not realize what they have until late in life. Some don't even realize it at all!

Empathy is inherited

Being an empath is genetic and inherent in our DNA as people. However, the ability isn't always developed in people. It can be studied and tapped into with consistent practice, of course. Empathy, itself, has both biological and spiritual aspects. Empaths can sense energy / emotion in differing ways as well.

2 - Different Levels of Being an Empath

As established earlier, there are many different kinds of empaths and they perceive the energy around them in varying ways as well. Here are the ten levels of empathy that people may fall under:

Psychometry

This is a person's ability to receive impressions, energy and even information from photographs, objects, as well as places.

Telepathy

This is a person's ability to read another person's thoughts. Most would be familiar with this as it has been portrayed in both literature and film countless times.

Physical Healing

This is a person's ability to actually sense any physical symptoms in another. In some cases, they would also have the ability to transmute or heal said symptoms.

Emotional Healing

This a person's ability to feel another's emotions; particularly, the deep ones that they may tend to hide. They are able to sense if someone is being weighed down by something and are also capable of helping with easing that burden.

Animal Communication

This is a person's ability to hear an animal's thoughts, feel their emotions, and even communicate with them mentally.

Nature

This is a person's ability to communicate with nature and plants. This includes allowing them to better tend to the ones that they keep.

Precognition

This is a person's ability to feel when something important is about to happen. You can think of this as that inexplicable restlessness that you cannot shake off.

Claircognizance

This is a person's ability to feel, knowing what has to be done given any circumstance. It is a kind of calmness despite being in the midst of chaos.

3 - Common Empathic Traits

Knowing

One of the first things you'll notice about empathic people is their ability to just "know" things even without having been told about it prior. It's a kind of knowing that is beyond what we often refer to as intuition or gut feel this is because their certainty and accuracy tends to be impeccable when it comes to this.

Needless to say, you'd have a hard time lying to one. The more in tune they become with their gift, the better they come at reading energies.

For an empathic person, being in a public space can be very overwhelming. Places such as stadiums, shopping malls, and supermarkets can fill them with different emotions often leading them to simply stay away. Remember, empaths are like emotional sponges and their sensitivity is far greater than that of the average person, therefore, they feel a whole lot more.

Describing an empath as a kind of emotional sponge isn't too far-off how they really are. The thing is that they feel other people's emotions and take those feelings as their own. This is why some of them tend to dislike the gift.

After all, can you imagine going through such a thing on a daily basis? It can be exhausting. Of course, this varies depending on how adept the empathic person is. For the most part, they will still feel people's emotions and this can affect them either negatively or positively.

Watching violence or anything tragic on the television can sometimes be unbearable for them. There are empaths who find it difficult to even read the newspaper as they become overwhelmed with emotion each time they do. This is something that empathic people cannot help.

They can easily tell whenever someone is lying or being insincere. There's that expression: "Ignorance is bliss" and for many empaths, this rings true. If a loved one lies to them, the pain they feel is double for they cannot help what they know.

It isn't just feelings that empaths can pick up from another person. They can also "absorb" ailments off of other people illnesses such as colds, infections and even body pain. This is especially so if the sick person is someone they love dear. The empath ends up developing the same symptoms as the other person. Think of it as something similar to "sympathy pains".

Physically, most empaths would also often have lower back problems, as well as digestive issues. This is where empathic people would be able to feel the emotion of another and in time, it begins to weaken too.

When that happens and it is left untreated, it can lead to stomach ulcers and IBS. Problems with the lower back tend to happen when the person is ungrounded or have no knowledge of even having the ability. There are ways of healing this, however, so don't fret. We shall get to those later.

They always look out for other people, particularly the underdogs and those who they know to be in emotional pain. They cannot help but feel drawn to them and given that empaths are capable of sharing these hidden pains, they also make for some of the best friends you'll ever meet.

That said, they also often become the people who others feel most comfortable opening up to. They have an always ready to listen ear, but the danger here is that if they aren't careful, those problems others may share with them can end up becoming their own.

They are almost, always exhausted. This is the inevitable result of them taking on too much from other people, whether it be voluntarily or involuntarily. Self-care is very important for empathic people, lest they end up burning themselves to the ground by absorbing too much, and too often from other people.

You may think that empaths, given their heightened self-awareness, would be much less prone to vices. However, this isn't true for everyone.

Many empaths tend to have addictive personalities; they are prone to developing dependencies on drugs, alcohol, and even sex. This is a way for them to block out the emotions they unconsciously absorb from others. Think of it as a form of self-protection, but a potentially harmful one.

Most empathic people are also drawn to various forms of healing, the metaphysical, and holistic therapies. For those who are aware of their abilities, they often find joy in healing others, but would often turn away from becoming healers themselves. Are there doctors who are empathic?

That is a possibility, but given the nature of the work and the environment some doctors are placed in, the likelihood is pretty slim. Of course, another reason could be that empaths are drawn to all things supernatural a doctor would be bound by the laws of medicine and science, something that empathic people might find too limiting.

They are very creative. From writing, singing, acting, dancing or drawing, most empaths would have a creative streak not to mention, a very vivid and extensive imagination. This could be attributed to the unique way they experience things; enabling them to have more insight and a deeper understanding of beauty as well.

Empaths tend to be nature loves and find that being in it is the best cure for their lingering feelings of fatigue. Most of them would keep pets as well and they end up forming very strong, familial bonds with the animals they care for.

Empaths love people, but all the same, they also have a deep need for solitude. They will always require their quiet time and this need does not change even with age. Both adult and children empaths tend to become moody or very restless if they don't get some time alone.

They tend to get distracted easily if they're doing something that isn't very interesting to them if it does not stimulate them enough. Boredom sets in very quickly for empaths as well and they are very prone to rumination.

It would be impossible for them to do something that they cannot derive any form of joy from. This makes them feel less authentic and as if they're not fulfilling their potential as people. In some cases, empaths do tend to get labelled as "lazy", simply because there's no way a person would be able to force them to do something they dislike.

So what catches an empath's attention? Typically, this involves the search for answers and knowledge. They are very curious people and many enjoy learning more about their ability and how it might be of better use to them, as well as others. They always have questions, but take it upon themselves to find the answer.

Are empaths timid people? Some are, some aren't. Most would be free spirits, however. They enjoy traveling and feeling every experience with intensity. These people are staunch advocates of living freely and saying yes to adventures that come knocking on their door.

You may think that an empath, given that they are prone to daydreaming and having rather chaotic minds, would be disorganized people, but this is not the case at all. In fact, many of them abhor clutter finding that it can actually block the proper flow of energy and only adds to them feeling weighed down.

Many empaths are intolerant towards a lot of things, this is one of the reasons why some people often find them either: too sensitive, too judgmental or simply hard to understand. However, being judgmental is far from what they actually are.

They simply cannot tolerate attitudes that most people simply brush aside. For example, they cannot stand narcissism and would often point this out as well out of consideration for the person, and other people.

An empath who is adept when it comes to their ability may also feel the different days of the week. Some would get something like a "Friday Feeling"; most of the time, this is what the collective around them is feeling. If everyone at work is excited, even if they don't show it or speak it, the empath would be able to feel that energy.

The same goes for negative energy as well; if everyone at work is feeling bogged down and then the empath would sense this and carry it around for the duration of the week or until the mood around them changes.

For empaths who are capable of reading energy from objects, it is likely that they would refuse or avoid buying vintage, antiques or secondhand items. Anything that has a residual energy which they can end up absorbing.

However, there are the curious ones who enjoy this; finding the experience to be like time-traveling as they get to "relieve" certain periods of time through an object and the energy imprinted upon it by the previous owner.

The same goes for empaths who can also sense the energy in their food. Some would refuse to eat any type of they meat as they can often feel the vibration of the animal (particularly so if the animal suffered in any way).

At first glance, most empaths would appear disconnected, moody, and aloof. Of course, this all depends on how they are feeling as well, but these people would never put on a mask to hide their emotions from the world. They are most prone to mood swings as this can be directly influenced by the energy they happen to absorb.

If they have taken on too much negative energy, they will

become very unsociable and appear miserable. This is because they refuse to pass on the negative energy to another person, but there are instances wherein others might misinterpret these actions as disinterest.

One of the biggest challenges an empath might face when it comes to forming relationships is trying to explain why they feel a certain way to other people. Not everyone would be able to easily understand how their ability works and there would always be those people who would even reject the very existence of it.

The latter is also one of the reasons why an empathic person might begin to hold themselves back, not wanting to be thought of as different and be treated as an outsider. Bottling up their emotions can actually be detrimental to an empath's physical and mental health. The more they do it, the greater the frustration they feel.

So, what can they do to protect and take better care of themselves?

4 - Being Empathic and the Ability to Heal

The gift of being empathic is certainly a blessing, but it comes with a lot of challenges. Imagine being able to sense the feelings, and even the thoughts of those around you. If they happen to be very positive then it wouldn't be that bad, right?

Now, picture the same thing happening, but with everyone's energies going in every direction. Happy, miserable, excited, nervous all of these things add up and can easily overwhelm an empath. It can make them feel physically ill, in some instances.

What if you had to go through that experience nearly every single day? What if you didn't really have anyone who understood your ability and would often misinterpret your actions instead?

It's quite sad, isn't it? This is the reality that most, if not all, empaths face. These things can easily cause them to detach themselves from others, preferring solitude as it is easier on them mentally and physically. However, that is no way to live, right?

This is why self-healing is important for empathic people. It is a way for them to detoxify and clear their head after a long day. After all, they get drained very easily of energy and would need to re-energize more often than the rest of us.

5 - What to Avoid if you are an empath

There is no doubt that withholding their emotions can be very detrimental towards an empath's health. The longer they do this, the more power these unreleased emotions and thoughts have. In time, they may become crippling.

If they aren't given the opportunity to express themselves honestly or are somehow withheld from it by another, this can result in a breakdown mental, as well as emotional instability which may manifest itself physically as well. Heart ailments are common in empathic people.

Aside from this, empaths should also try and limit their exposure to triggering stimuli. They can be very sensitive to TV shows that portray violence; particularly those that inflict physical and emotional pain to children, adults, and even animals.

Where some people would often cry, empaths can start feeling physically ill because of what they're being presented with. One of the main reasons for this is the fact that empaths do struggle to understand such cruelty and lack of compassion.

6 - Self-Care for Empathic People

Whilst there are things that can be avoided, there are plenty more that empaths have no choice but learn how to cope with. This is where the importance of self-healing becomes of value. There are many ways to do this, but here are a few everyday things that empathic people can practice in order to keep themselves from becoming drained by those around them:

Practice gratefulness meditation for at least twenty minutes each day. What this does is trigger the release of feel good hormones which would then balance out a number of stress hormones in our body. By doing this, you'd be able to regulate your heart beat and feel a lot less restless and anxious.

Make sure you get enough sleep each time. When you're sleepless, the mind is actually more vulnerable and the harder it would be for you to create a calm boundary around yourself. You also get more irritable which makes you more likely to start feeling negative energy.

Do manage your exposure to certain media properly. As much as possible, limit yourself when it comes to reading up on the day's news. However, if you'd rather not shield yourself when learning about world events (this matters greatly!), then make sure that you try and balance the negativity with something positive. Watch videos that make you smile or listen to music that calms you down.

Start decluttering your surroundings. Begin with the bedroom as this is where most people tend to keep things that mean a lot of them; if you find objects that carry unresolved emotional stories in them, do your best to start letting go.

Holding on to these can only increase negative energy around you and this is what you must seek to avoid. After you finish with one area, continue on and move to the next until you feel much lighter.

Do your best to avoid drama. This means that you should avoid people around you with are very gossipy. Do the same things with people who make you feel small and unwanted. Continuously hanging out with this kind of crowd can really bring your energy level down you don't need that. Protect your energy better and you'll really feel a lot lighter about yourself as well.

Whenever you start feeling overwhelmed to the point of exhaustion, always ask yourself: "Is this emotion mine?" For empaths, it is likely that the answer is NO. You are merely absorbing someone else's energy and feeling exactly the way they are in that moment.

Acknowledging this fact really does help when it comes to diminishing its effects. Once you understand that the energy isn't yours, you can begin to slowly detach yourself from it and restore your own. It might take a while, however, but meditation will certainly hasten the process.

Start learning how to say NO to people. The thing with empathic people is that they often feel quite guilty after saying no. Some would even feel as if it is their purpose to share some of the world's energy burden they want to fix things but want to avoid it simultaneously.

If you ever find yourself too overwhelmed to the point that you feel paralyzed by it; refuse and say no more. It is important to take care of yourself first before anyone else.

Spend some time outdoors. It needn't be somewhere far, like going into the mountains to camp. You can opt to go for short walks outside, especially if the weather is particularly good. Find a nice grassy spot where you can stand barefoot on the ground.

Do this for at least ten minutes a day whilst you practice

gratefulness meditation. By connecting to the earth, you are actually grounding yourself and renewing any lost energy. This practice has been proven to be very effective.

Make sharing joy and laughter a daily practice. Here's a fact: Laughing really does wonders for our physical and mental health. Do something that brings you joy on a daily basis. No matter how simple it is taking some time off to work on a hobby, treating yourself to your favorite food or spending time with people you love. It is important to step out of a negative frame of mind and change your routine a little.

7 - Energy Techniques for the Intuitive Feeler

Aside from the more practical ways that an empath can use to protect their energy, there are other more metaphysical techniques that they can use as a means of defending and stabilizing said energy. The idea here is to not shut out everyone else's energy. Instead one simply learns how to filter what they allow in. This also gives you more control over your ability.

To help you get started, here are two easy to follow techniques which you can practice whenever you feel the need to create a barrier between yourself and any unwanted energies in your surroundings.

The Zip Up

This one was created by Donna Eden. Visualize an energy cape or coat that you slip on in order to protect you against absorbing another person's energy this is what the Zip Up technique is meant to do.

Basically, it works with your central meridian, also known as the energy pathway which moves along the center line of your torso. This controls your central nervous system as well.

For many people, not just empaths, this central meridian often acts like a rod that channels the energy, thoughts, and feelings of the people around you. Whilst this is alright in some cases, you must also know how to properly protect yourself in order to avoid becoming overwhelmed.

In doing this, many empaths say that they feel more positive and renewed. They were also able to think with more clarity and tap into their own inner strength, shielding themselves from any negative build up in their environment.

To do it

1. Begin by placing your hand or both of your hands on the very bottom of your central meridian. This is located at the top of your pubic bone, facing up the body.

2. Follow this up with a deep breath, let go of any tension in your body. As you do this, move your hands up the center of your body, all the way to your lower lip. You can also opt to do this with your hands touching your body or a few inches away from it. Try your best to focus on what you're doing and if you're distracted, pause then take another breath before

continuing.

3. You can repeat this practice for up to three times or whenever you feel as if it is needed.

Creating a Shield of Light

This one is meant to create a boundary between you and energy that you are trying to avoid. It will keep unwanted feelings and thoughts at bay, as well as help with clearing your energy field. This is particularly great for people who need more room to breathe, psychologically and energetically.

If you work in an environment where everyone's energies seem to bombard you all the time, this would be a great practice to do. It involves a degree of visualization so you might want to find a quiet space for this.

To do it

1. Begin by visualizing yourself being enveloped by a blanket of light. Imagine it wrapping around you like a shield, not quite touching your body but near enough. This is your own energy field manifesting physically. If you can, try to imagine what it feels like. Warm, cozy something that makes you feel very se-

cure.

2. Next, bring your elbows closer to your sides, keeping both palms facing outward. Breathe in deep and slowly breathe out as you slowly push both hands outwards; while you do this, visualize that you are spreading your light shield further as well.

The more you can focus on this picture, and really feel it, the more effective this exercise will be. It will take a few tries, but with constant use, you will get the hang of it.

3. Remember that there is no need to rush this step. Go as slowly as needed. As you push outwards, visualize the shield of light expanding, the pressure of it against your palms, and how it's pushing away the energy that does not belong to you. Visualize all of the negative energy fading against the strength of your own light shield. Focus on that image as you breathe in and out slowly.

4. Follow this with a period of rest. Put your arms down comfortably at your sides and focus now on your breathing. Let the feeling of lightness fill you. Breathe

in and out slowly once more before moving on to your other tasks.

5. You can repeat this exercise whenever needed. However, it is best done in a place where you can have some quiet and without worrying about any time constraints.

Belly Breathing

As you may have noticed breathing plays a fairly central role when it comes to these exercises. This is because proper breathing can really help remove tension from the body and enable the mind to focus on the present.

Most of us have a tendency to breathe shallowly and rapidly, keeping it all in our chests. This is fine, but to reach that meditative state, you would want to breathe in deeply. For this, belly breathing is the best especially for the intuitive feeler. Why?

- It helps ground you, making you more in tune with your emotions and body.

- It helps center you.

- It can restore vitality, especially if you're feeling burnout.

- It can relieve anxiety and ease tense nerves.

Every chance you get, try slowing down your breathing and making sure that the air moves into the lower third of your lungs. You'll know that you're doing things right if your belly rises up each time you inhale and fall as you breathe out. There is a chance that you might feel light-headed, especially if this is your first time, simply return to your usual breathing pattern until you feel better again.

Once you do get the hang of it, try to incorporate breathing exercises into your daily routine. It need not eat up so much time; five minutes a day should be fine to center you again especially if you're going through a stressful time.

You can even do it while you're at work, at school, or even while you're out and anxiety starts kicking in. The bottom line is, this type of breathing is good for you physically, mentally and emotionally.

8 - Lifestyle Changes for Empaths

Aside from incorporating meditative practices into your daily routine, you can also opt to make lifestyle modifications which can help you maximize your gifts, whilst minimizing the energy draining effects it has on you. Here are a few simple ideas to help you get started:

Start with avoiding people whose energies are toxic to yours. There are those who will purposely manufacture drama in their lives and these are the people you need to stay away from. Try and keep your circle filled with upbeat friends, as well as people who are stable and optimistic.

Another thing you should avoid would be any form of media that affects you adversely. This includes books, unfortunately, as there are certain ones which can trigger ill feelings in many empaths.

It would be god to do a bit of research before purchasing a book or watching a movie this would help you avoid wasting money on something that you won't end up enjoying. Reviews would be very useful for this purpose.

As much as you can, spend plenty of time in nature. Plants are actually great buffers for your emotions and the environment immediately puts you in a more relaxed mood.

Treat yourself to getaways a bit more often, even if it's just a quick trip to the country or a garden close to your home.

Do not be afraid of doing things on your own. Most empaths recover better whenever they spend time by themselves. However, not everyone is very comfortable with this solitude. Think about the reason why you're not comfortable and do your best to get better acquainted with this side of you. Your mind will be thanking you for it.

Be more aware of the places you frequent that aren't good for your overall energy. This differs for every empath so a need to be more observant is needed. If you can, avoid these places. Explain to your friends why you cannot stay very long in that area, and suggest other ones that they might enjoy more.

If you explain your needs well enough, they should be able to easily understand the discomfort that being in that environment is giving you.

Be better at handling conflict. Conflict is inevitable chances are, you will never grow to like it. However, you can start managing it better. A counselor would be helpful for this purpose, but if you would rather try and provide a solution to the matter on your own, then there are plenty of self-help books that could give you more insight into it. Just research, you'll find exactly what you need in time.

Most empaths tend to choose professions where they can help other people think teaching, counseling, coaching, and healing. For empaths who are in these particular fields, it is important that you remember self-care.

Learn how to use your energy for yourself. Use the meditation practices previously provided, take some time off to restore your vitality put the same amount of care you give to others unto yourself. You'll be better at your job too!

Look around your personal space. Is everything organized? Is it clutter-free? A clean environment breeds a clear mind. If you can, always keep your surroundings organized. This lessens the amount of things you need to be anxious about and provides you with a calm place to rest your mind in. Remember, your home must be your sanctuary so treat it as such.

Here's a fact: Despite an empath's efforts to create limits between themselves and energy vampires, there will always be an "emotional hangover" that could happen. This refers to the residual energy left behind by a previous interaction.

Negative energy tends to linger a lot longer than others, often leaving an empath feeling ill or lacking clarity. In some cases, especially if an empath deals with energy vampires on a daily basis, it would take them a lot of time to recuperate.

So, what can they do in this situation? Well, cleanse themselves of the bad energy is a start. There are many different ways of curing emotional hangovers it really depends on the situation and what the person really needs as well. To help you better understand this and to give you an idea about how to cure emotional hangovers, here are a few strategies to get you started:

9 - Tips for Curing Emotional Hangovers

Shower meditation

If you have enough time during the mornings or during the weekends, use your time in the shower to help cleanse you of any negative energy that might linger. Stay under the shower head and the let water stream from the top of your head all the way to your feet; as this happens, recite the affirmation:

"This water will cleanse all the negative energy from my body, my mind, and my spirit." As you repeat it, visualize that bad energy leaving you. Repeat it until you start feeling lighter. By the end of it, you will feel a lot more rejuvenated.

In continuing with cleansing and adjusting your space to meet your needs, try using salt lamps as well as negative ion generators. What these would do is produce negative ions which then clears the environment of different pollutants such as mold spores, dust, pollen, odors, viruses, cigarette smoke and different types of bacteria.

Light a white-colored candle.

This is especially useful when you're meditation or simply unwinding after a long day. This creates a calming mood and also helps in removing negativity your surroundings.

Aromatherapy

Take advantage of the soothing effects that aromatherapy has. Rosewater is a favorite among many people, but choose the scent you feel most comfortable with. You can use sprays or synthetic oils which you'll need to add to diffusers in order to spread the aroma around. You can even choose purifying scents such as frankincense, myrrh and sage.

Nature

We've already established how effective being in nature can be if you want to ground yourself. Earthing takes this one step further and actually connects you to the ground first, take your shoes off and stand barefoot on the ground. Do this while your practice both visual and breathing meditation.

You'll find that focusing on nothing but the sound of your breath really helps clear the mind of any negative thoughts.

The earth, with its own natural energy, will replenish yours the longer you stay grounded to it.

Create your sanctuary.

If you live with other people, it is important to create a safe space for yourself. You'll need this if you want to properly meditate and keep any distractions at bay. It need not be an entire room. In fact, even a corner of your bedroom would work just as fine as long as it has the basics: incense, candles, flowers, and a totem that you can focus your gaze on while you meditate.

Now, when should you practice some of these tips? There need not be a "time" for it. These are basically small lifestyle changes you can add to your everyday life. Things that you can turn to whenever the emotional hangover becomes a little too burdensome for you.

As an empath, you'll find that this will happen a lot. So, instead of only acting when the problem arises, always be one step ahead and prepare for the situation.

10 - Empaths and the Workplace

Now, let's talk about the workplace. Sure, some empaths do have it easier than others are able to choose a suitable job for the empathic person. For the most part, the basic needs are simple it just has to be fulfilling and stress-free.

A job that maximizes their gifts is great too, something that many empaths would often go after. A job that provides them with an outlet for their quiet nature, creativity and intuition is highly recommended.

Some of the best careers for empaths would be those where they need to deal with only a few people. Most of them would be happiest in smaller companies or working from home where they have more control over who they interact with. Office intrigue isn't something that an empath would enjoy nor partake in.

Freelancing is also another option as it enables them to meet new people, but still have control over it. Flexibility in a job is a very important consideration, especially when it comes to time as they would need regular breaks in order to recover lost energy.

Many would choose self-employment for this reason, as it enables them to avoid the pressure of needing to deal with office hierarchy. If they can work within their own time, even better! Rigid schedules are not their thing and they perform better if they can work at their own pace.

There are empaths that do thrive in an office environment as well. However, this depends on a number of different conditions. For example, if the people surrounding them are all relatively positive this energy motivates an empath.

Which jobs are empaths drawn to? Well, whenever they opt to be self-employed, you'll find that empaths do excellent as editors, writers, artists, medical professionals, and any job in the creative field.

Other career options include: graphic and website design, accountants, lawyers with private practices, virtual assist-ants, independent plumbers and electricians all of whom are capable of setting up their own schedule.

There would be those who can even do well in business con-sulting and real estate; however, they need to be able to work at their own pace as well. Those with a keenness for nature would do well as forest rangers, landscape designers, as well as horticulturists.

As mentioned earlier, there are also those who prefer taking on professions wherein they can help other people. Many empaths often choose to become social workers, teachers, nurses, therapists anything that brings them closer to others in order to provide some degree of healing.

Some do well in animal rescue and non-profit organizations; all of which are very fulfilling jobs, something that an empath is drawn to. Of course, these are also careers that can be highly stressful, and as such, an empath would need to learn how to protect them from being consumed by work. Regular breaks would be necessary so they can refuel.

It is necessary for empaths to feel stimulated by the job they have chosen. Their skills should be put to use and their talents, maximized. Sure, they may not be the type to thrive in big corporations, professional sports, academia, the military, and government duties, but they can still contribute greatly to whichever career they decide to take on.

The thing with empaths is that they know themselves very well they know what they can do and how that can help. They are full of energy if they love what they're doing, if it is a job they're completely passionate about. For these people, money is just cherry on top of the cake. Their personal needs must be met first. Impractical, yes, but this is simply how these people function. Passion above all else!

Alright, now that we have possible careers outlined, let's talk about what are some of the jobs that an empath should avoid? Now, this doesn't mean that they would be incapable in these jobs. Rather, it only points to the high level of stress and energy demand that these jobs entails things that may not be healthy for an empath and may cause them to feel exhausted quickly. Many of these jobs also undermine their empathic nature.

One such profession would be sales. Given that this is a very extroverted job in nature, empaths might find it difficult to keep up. This is especially so if they encounter aggressive clients. Keep in mind that empaths, such as yourself, do absorb the energy from the environment you're in. If you encounter a number of rowdy people all day long, you will end up drained and burnt out.

The same applies to jobs in politics, public relations, as well as executive work where dealing with large groups of people is a constant. These are jobs that don't really require introspection or sensitivity instead, it's all talk and talk. Aggressively pushing products and ideas forward are things that empaths don't do too well at.

Corporate work is a big no-no for them. The mentality within the environment of big corporations can be extremely exhausting for empaths. These are places that do not give much value to an individual's needs and output is of great importance.

There is a rigid structure that must be followed; schedules, deadlines these are things that many empaths seek to avoid. Their lifestyle and way of thing wouldn't fit in well with it.

That said, there are certain times when an empath might not be able to avoid being in a job that they don't necessarily like. Everyone has to live and money is a factor in that, right? So, what can they do to improve their situation whilst taking advantage of their inherent skill? It's learning how to adapt to the environment. Learning how to read people can be important as well in order to avoid unnecessary confrontations.

To help with that, here are three simple techniques that you can try:

Observing Body Language Cues.

Research shows that words can only account for about 7% of how we communicate. Body language, on the other hand, accounts for about 55%, whilst voice tone comes in at 30%. Now, how is this useful? For empaths, this would be useful in determining if the person they're speaking to is genuinely interested in their conversation.

They can take certain movements as cues as to where they should nudge the topic towards. That said, this can lead to them becoming too analytical as well so find a balance. Instead of focusing too much on how the person is reacting, just stay fluid and relax.

Be comfortable and stay true to yourself. Do not try too hard to get the person to show interest nor should you feel bad if it happens that they are not always reacting positively.

Pay Attention to Appearance

Ask yourself, what is the first thing you notice when you meet other people for the first time? It is likely that you first pay attention to what they're wearing before moving on to any other feature. Are they dressed properly? Do they look shabby?

We tend to gather our first impression of someone based upon how they look. If a person is well-dressed, we immediately associate that with a healthy well being. On the other hand, if a person looks shabby then we tend to see them as unhealthy or someone who is untrustworthy.

Notice Posture

Another thing we unconsciously pay attention to is a person's posture. How confident do they look? Do they look shy or are they cowering as you speak to them? These are also keys to their personality as well as how comfortable they feel around you. Next time you speak with someone, observe where their hands are. If it's folded across their chest, this is a sign of defensiveness or wariness.

On the other hand, if their arms are comfortably placed somewhere around their body, in their pockets for example, then this means they're quite comfortable with speaking to you. People who are like this tend to be more open conversationalists as well.

Watch For Physical Movements

Observe the way people lean and the distance at which they do. The idea here is that people lean forward or towards people we like whilst we lean away from people we are not too fond of.

As mentioned earlier, crossed arms and legs are both signs of defensiveness. In some cases, they could also point to anger or self-protection. Another thing to look for is where people point their toes at most individuals would point their toes towards the person they feel most comfortable with.

Pay attention to people's hands

When people have their hands on their laps, in their pockets or behind their back, this suggests that they might be hiding something. Whilst this isn't always an accurate observation, it is stills something that you should try and pay more attention to.

Lip biting

Whenever people do this, it is their way of soothing themselves under pressure or after a rather awkward encounter/situation. The same applies to cuticle picking observe children who have a habit of doing this. They tend to be some of the shyest ones.

Interpreting Facial Expressions

Emotions can sometimes be easily read upon people's faces. Frowning suggests worry or overthinking. Pursed lips might mean contempt, anger, or bitterness. Crow's feet could point to the fact that this person is quite jolly, often smiling and simply easygoing. A clenched jaw, however, can signal tension.

Listen to Your Intuition.

It might take some practice, but you can develop the skill of being able to tune into someone's energy beyond simply reading their language and words. This is where your intuitiveness will come in handy. Intuition is what your gut feels as opposed to what your head says.

Bear in mind that there is a difference between the two. This is the nonverbal information which you perceive through images and not by logic. If you truly want to understand a person, what really counts is who they are inside and not their outward appearance. Your intuition enables you to unravel the depth to a person one which others may not be able to easily see. This is your gift, after all.

Checklist of Intuitive Cues

Trust your gut feeling. When it comes to first meetings, listening to your gut is key given your gift of being able to feel people's energy. For most empaths, a first meeting is more than enough for them to be able to tell if they would be able to comfortably spend time with a person or not.

In fact, some of them can have a visceral reaction to negativity, allowing them to steer away from a potentially harmful friendship. So, listen to your gut feel as this serves as your internal truth meter.

Pay attention to how your body reacts to certain interactions. In particular, observe whenever your goosebumps rise up. These are physical manifestations of energy and can be great intuitive signals that can convey information when it comes to how people move us. They tend to happen during moments of some importance, whether we realize it or not, so be more aware of their appearances.

Have you ever had an "aha!" moment? Now, for most people, they may dismiss this as nothing of value, but for empaths pay more attention whenever this happens. These are moments that could provide you with great insight into the person you're speaking to or simply the current environment you are in. These things tend to happen in a flash, however, so if you're not very alert then you can easily miss it.

As mentioned earlier, some empaths are actually capable of physically feeling another person's symptoms and emotions. Think about it, whilst you're reading people, have you ever had stabbing pain somewhere in your body?

Did a meeting with someone leave you with a tingle and an unshakable positive feeling? Speak to the person you're with, ask them if they're feeling any pain this is how you'll be able to confirm if this is a result of your empathy or something else entirely.

Sense Emotional Energy

Emotions are an expression of our overall energy. This is the vibe we give off to other people and the same ones they project onto us. Have you encountered people who simply feel really good to be around with? The energy they give off is full of vitality and they can easily improve your mood.

On the other hand, you have others who can be draining and make you want to move away from them. As subtle as these energy projections are, empaths can easily pick up on them given their inherent sensitivity to it.

11 - Strategies to Read Emotional Energy

Sense People's Presence

Presence refers to the overall energy that we emit. This, however, isn't always related to their behavior and words. Imagine it as something that surrounds people like a cloud over their heads or a light around them. It's the atmosphere that they carry around them. Ask yourself this: Does the person you're speaking with have a friendly presence? Are they colder or distant?

Watch people's eyes

There is a reason why people say that the eyes are the windows to our souls this is because they can also transmit powerful energies. Just as our brains have electromagnetic signals that can extend beyond our body, there are studies that show how they eyes have this as well. So, when you're reading people, take some time to observe their eyes.

What kind of energy is it giving off? Understanding? Caring? Angry? Some empaths can sense whenever a person's guard is up by simply looking them in the eye. They can tell if the person is burdened by something or if they're hiding something heavy in their souls.

Notice the feel of a handshake, hug, and touch

Pay more attention to how a person's touch, handshake, and hug feels. We all share emotional energy by means of physical content; it can be comparable to a subtle electrical current. So, if you're meeting someone new, observe how physical contact with them makes you feel.

Is the handshake comfortable? Did it leave you with a feeling of warmth? Or did you feel shaken by it? Did the other person appear confident or timid? These are a few important key points to keep in mind.

Listen for people's laughter and tone of voice

A person's tone and the volume at which they speak can signal a number of things about their emotions. This is because sound frequencies also create vibrations. Observe how people's tone affects you whenever they speak. Does it feel soothing? Abrasive? You can learn of a few things about how they might be feeling at the given moment or how they feel about you just by listening to how they speak.

12 - The Connection Between Diet and Empathy

Do you tend to experience digestive issues often? IBS or an upset stomach? Are you sensitive when it comes to certain foods? Do you tend to have an aversion towards smoking, drinking alcohol, and taking prescription drugs?

If you answered yes to most of those questions don't fret. These are actually common things that many empaths tend to experience. Think about it: you process the energy you absorb through your energy centers, which are some of the most subtle parts of your body.

Every single day, you go through this, and the energy you absorb won't always be positive. In time, it all accumulates, and gets integrated into your system. This often leads to issues which can manifest physically as symptoms of various illnesses.

So why do empaths have sensitive bodies, and systems?

For the most part, this can be attributed to an actual lack of information about what is good for an empath and what they ought to avoid. Health and fitness aren't always top concerns for empaths, as they focus more on their mental health instead. However, as we've already established, every aspect of our body and self is interconnected.

Most empaths tend to abuse their bodies, eating and doing things which are detrimental to their overall well-being. Some turn to food as a means of comforting themselves after a challenging day, others might even use alcohol as a way of turning down the overwhelming feeling within them.

This, however, is the wrong way of doing things.

Empaths must learn how to better care for their health and how to strengthen their bodies. A strong body equals a strong mind both things that you need in order to overcome many of the challenges that come with your gift.

Just as much as you listen to other people's worries and problems, you must also learn how to listen to your own body. Listen to your system. Tune in to the subtle signs that your body is giving you and start doing things that would boost its overall health.

Did You know that eating the right food can keep your mind healthy as well? You eat certain food to improve your heart health, lower the risk of diabetes, and certain cancers but were you aware that the same can be said for improving your focus, memory, and overall brain function?

A few simple dietary changes can make you less susceptible to mood swings and help you focus better. There are food items that can lower anxiety and help you avoid falling into depression.

Remember, what you eat can also affect how your brain functions so always include brain-boosters in your diet. Here are a few examples of what you should routinely have:

Fatty Fish

An average person's typical diet would often lack important omega-3 fatty acids and is, instead, high in trans and saturated fats which are known to produce negative effects on the brain.

Consider the fact that or brains are largely made up of fat, and the fact that the body cannot manufacture its own supply of essential fatty acids, then it only goes that we need to rely on a daily supply of omega-3 fatty acids in order to meet our needs.

Whole Grains

When it comes to brain fuel, our primary source for this would be glucose which comes from carbs. However, it is of importance that you choose complex carbs for this as simple carbohydrates are known to actually create spikes in our blood sugar level. Healthy sources of glucose include whole wheat products, oats, bulgur, wild rice, soy, beans, and barley.

Lean Protein

Next to carbs, protein is another substance that's abundant in our bodies. Tryptophan, a building block of protein, actually influences our moods by helping produce serotonin. Now, for the unfamiliar, serotonin is commonly referred to as nature's Prozac and is also well known to help curb the effects of depression.

Some of the best lean protein sources available include eggs, chicken, beans, fish, and turkey. These would help keep serotonin levels in the body properly balanced. Coupled with complex carbs, they facilitate the flow of tryptophan into the brain, helping reduce the symptoms of anxiety, depression, and improves overall cognitive functions.

Leafy Greens

Alright, so veggies aren't exactly everyone's favorite but after you learn of their benefits, especially fr your mental health, you might change your mind about excluding them from your diet. Let's start with the basics these leafy greens are high in folic acid. Now, why does that matter?

Well, any deficiency in folate, as well as other B vitamins, is actually associated with depression, insomnia, and fatigue. As an empath, these are three things that you need to avoid at all costs.

Selenium is also another important component when it comes to relieving the symptoms of fatigue and anxiety. This can be readily found in broccoli as well as walnuts, onions, chicken, seafood, and brazil nuts.

Mood Foods: How Amino Acids Feed Your Brain

We've established the importance of getting a sufficient supply of amino acids to the brain, but not quite how it helps in boosting its overall functions. The four key mood chemicals, also known as neurotransmitters, are made up of amino acids. Protein-rich foods such as fish, beef, chicken, and eggs contain all twenty two types of amino acids.

Now, including these into your daily diet can help with:

- Boost your mood

- Kick starting the brain's repair job

- Frees you from cravings which sometimes results as an emotional response

It might seem as if restoring depleted brain chemistry is too big of a job for a single supplement, but you'd be surprised to know that this isn't the case. This is because three out of the four neurotransmitters that significantly affect your moods is comprised of a single amino acid each. Biochemists have successfully isolated these key amino acids, allowing you to add the ones you specifically need to your diet.

Studies confirm the effectiveness of using these targeted amino acids to help increase the amount of neurotransmitters in our body which, in turn, helps with eliminating depression, lowering anxiety levels, as well as decreasing cravings for alcohol, food, and even drugs/medication.

13 - Restoring Energy and Focus

One of the biggest things that empaths tend to struggle with is the lack of focus and the fact that their energy gets drained very easily; this is especially so if they are surrounded by negativity and their brain is inadequately fueled due to a bad diet. This makes them more vulnerable, so to speak.

Sure, a shot of caffeine can help, but too much of it can also be bad. Why not turn to something more natural then? L-Glutamine is often referred to as such. It is an all-natural brain stimulant that serves as a very potent brain fuel.

Without it, you will feel slow and have a harder time trying to focus and filter out any unwanted energy. It would also be harder for you to stay on track mentally this leaves many people feeling lethargic, which also puts them at risk of slipping into depression.

For empaths, making sure that your diet has plenty of this natural caffeine will be beneficial. Not just for your interaction with the people around you, but for being more productive when it comes to work as well.

Boosting Your Ability to Relax

Another thing that many empaths struggle with would be relaxing. One would think that after a long, tiring day of dealing with people, empaths would find it very easy to unwind and get into a more relaxed state of mind. However, this isn't always the case.

This is where GABA or Gamma Amino Butyric Acid enters the picture. Think of it as a natural valium which acts like a sponge, absorbing any excess adrenaline along with other by-products left by stress.

It is capable of draining the stiffness and tension out of our muscles, and is also known to help with smoothing out seizure activity in our brain. In fact, it is also given to heroin addicts who are going through severe anxiety following detoxification.

Needless to say, it is very effective when it comes to diminishing stress levels in the body and enabling empaths to feel more at ease.

Food vs. Comfort

It's no secret that there are people who use food as a means of comforting themselves. Some find that it produces drug-like results, allowing them to forget their worries for the time-being.

Many empaths are prone to this particular problem, using food to make themselves feel better. Food can often compensate for the depletion of endorphins in the body, something that affects empaths more than the average person.

Think about it this way, what they go through on a daily basis can seem intolerable after the effect of these endorphins fade. Food becomes a secondary source for it, however, and thus many turn to it. This results in overeating just to feel that temporary "high".

If you use food in this manner, you are using them in the same way as synthetic drugs. While this might seem harmless at first, the way it can adversely affect your health is a very real problem. It is addictive in the same way cocaine or heroin is, and can be just as damaging if not controlled.

Ask yourself, do you often find yourself wanting to eat more after an overwhelming day? Do you tend to pour out your feelings but binging on your favorite food?

Some people will treat this lightly even make a joke out of

doing it. However, it can become a real problem especially for empathic people who then start becoming dependent on the "feel good" effect that food has on them. Once that fades too, what happens? The crash happens.

Fortunately, nature provides us with safer alternatives.

Serotonin, the All-Natural Prozac

Did you know that one of the easiest deficiencies that people can develop is low serotonin levels in the body? This is a rather jarring thought given its function to make us feel good, content, and energetic. So, how does this happen? It really all boils down to the kind of diet we have.

There are very few foods that contain Tryptophan, the amino acid that enables the body to produce serotonin. If you're dieting, you're already at risk of developing low serotonin levels. It can also be genetic some people are simply preconditioned to have low amounts of it. Stress is yet another trigger for its decline, often making it fall to amounts so low that it can set off a number of emotional disturbances.

In fact, restoring proper levels of serotonin in your body can become a life or death matter. Again, empaths are most prone to this, but even the average person can experience its ill effects. Violent crimes and suicides are also closely associated with serotonin deficiency. The same applies to fatal obsessions, anorexics and the self-hate that bulimics experience.

For some people, it can be difficult to understand that symptoms such as fear, low self-esteem, and the need for control are all biochemical problems and not solely psychological ones. However, the use of Prozac and its success gives us insight to the more biochemical nature of these issues.

14 - Inspiring Change by Using Your Empathic Abilities

Cultivate Your Curiosity

It is inherent in empaths to be very curious about people. Some can find it quite easy to strike up a conversation with someone seated next to them on a bus, and be able to find simple connections that make the exchange beneficial for both people involved.

This is because empaths have also retained that inquisitiveness which came naturally to us as children, but one which society has all but erased in most others. This is also why some people tend to center the conversation on themselves, finding their own person more interesting than other. Empaths understand this on a deeper level.

The thing that's great about curiosity, whether you're empathic or not, is the fact that it truly expands your empathy towards others. You can learn plenty through it. You can encounter lives, stories, and people whose views are vastly different from your own.

It can open your eyes to something much bigger than yourself; this can become the key to happiness as well. By opening up your perspective, you start seeing that all your worries were for naught.

Cultivating curiosity is something that you slowly work yourself up to; yes, not every empath is capable of striking up a conversation out of the blue. For some it takes time. Try starting small.

Chatting about the weather can eventually move onto other topics, and help you understand the person you're speaking to. Think of people as stories, each one is different, each one is colorful. You simply have to turn the page and learn more about them. Connect with people.

Remember, in conversing, you must know how to listen and how to open up.

Step Into Someone Else's Shoes

Walk a mile in someone else's shoes before you judge them. Isn't that how the popular saying goes? Most people would find this difficult as there are many things that prevent them from empathizing with another.

For some, it's self-centeredness, and a belief that they are superior. For others, it's simply disinterest. Empaths are great at this, however. People like you are gifted with the ability to actually live another person's life.

Think deep-sea diving is an extreme sport? Well, what if you can gain a direct experience of it through others by making use of experiential empathy? Yes, it is one of the most challenging types of empathizing with others. However it is also one of the most rewarding depending on how you use it and on what.

Impossible? Not quite. Take George Orwell for example. After spending years as a colonial police officer in British Burma, he went home to Britain, absolutely determined to experienced what it was like for people who lived on the social margins.

He wanted to submerge himself, to discover what it was like for them. And that he did dressed as a tramp with a tattered coat and worn down shoes, the author lived on the streets of East London alongside vagabonds and beggars.

The result of which is what we find recorded in his book: Down and Out in Paris and London.

The experience brought about significant changes in his priorities, beliefs, and relationships. It opened his eyes to the fact that homeless people were not "scoundrels" as the rest of upper society would label them. Instead, he developed new friendships, gathered great material for his work, and radically changed his views on inequality.

In this manner, he was able to turn his empathy into something powerful, something that could inspire change not just within him, but to those around him.

Observe! Be more open to different experiences the more you open your eyes to the things you would have avoided, the more you'll learn about the world around you and your part in it.

Inspiring Social Change

Turn your weaknesses into strengths. Yes, being empathic is difficult, but there's also great strength in it. With a person's ability to empathize, the world would be in shambles; history's greatest movements would not have happened and we will be stuck in a world of barbaric beliefs where brute strength rules over the weak.

A good example of this would be the movements against slavery which began in the 18th and 19th centuries, on both sides of the Atlantic. It was a time when abolitionists put their faith, not in sacred texts, but in human empath. They did what they could so that people saw and understood the suffering within the slave ships and the plantations.

The International Trade Union also blossomed out of empathy between the workers who were united by their shared exploitation. That is strength.

More recent events such as the Asian tsunami of 2004 showed the way in which empathy can bring an entire world together to help the response was overwhelming, with even the poorest of nations providing what they could to those in need. That is strength. It helped with healing the wounds left by the event, it helped peopled find their way again.

Can you imagine living in a world where empathy does not exist? A world where it is frowned upon and hidden?

As difficult as it can be living as an empath, you must also recognize your own strength and how you can contribute to the whole. Whether it be by individual deeds or a collective effort, it is important that you recognize what you can do.

Acknowledge the gift and believe it is such.

Once you see yourself as something of value, healing would happen naturally. After all, the only way you can really help others is if you're capable of taking care of yourself first and foremost.

Thank You

As we reach the end of this book, I want to say thanks for reading this book.

I want to get this information out to as many people as possible. If you found this book helpful, I would greatly appreciate you leaving me a review. This helps others find the book as well.

Disclaimer

This document is geared towards providing exact and reliable information in regards to the topic and issue covered. The publication is sold on the idea that the publisher is not required to render an accounting, officially permitted, or otherwise, qualified services. If advice is necessary, legal, financial, medical or professional, a practiced individual in the profession should be ordered.

This information is not presented by a financial or medical practitioner and is for entertainment, educational and informational purposes only. The content is not intended as a substitute for professional medical advice, diagnosis, or treatment. Always seek the advice of your physician or other qualified health care provider with any questions you may have regarding a medical condition. Never disregard professional medical advice or delay in seeking it because of something you have read.

The information provided herein is stated to be truthful and consistent, in that any liability, in terms of inattention or otherwise, by any usage or abuse of any policies, processes, or directions contained within is the solitary and utter responsibility of the recipient reader. Under no circumstances will any legal responsibility or blame be held against the

DISCLAIMER

publisher for any reparation, damages, or monetary loss due to the information herein, either directly or indirectly.

Last Updated: 12.Jul.2017